The Core Question

Frank E Cahill

American Ink Paperbacks

ISBN-10: 1500582808
ISBN-13: 978-1500582807

ALSO BY FRANK E CAHILL

Malfeasance In Office

The Magic of Flying

CONTENTS

The start of my focused interest in the subjects of *The Core Question* began about 2009 during the Congressional debates concerning the need for health care insurance for all Americans, which eventually resulted with the Patient Protection and Affordable Care Act of 2010. It appeared that the country was headed for yet another human resources program that would force Americans to participate in it and support it, not unlike the Social Security and Medicare programs that preceded it. It was evident that federal spending on human resource programs would continue to grow without boundaries if the health care plan were implemented.

Listening to the comments of legislators, and seeing the tactics they used to pass the legislation finally became too much to bear. Various private organizations and advisors drafted the enormous legislative bill, so most of the elected legislature was unfamiliar with the details and provisions of the bill when it was brought to a vote. When the logic of a senior legislative leader encouraged the others to pass the bill quickly because it was sorely needed, and then find out what was in it later, I wondered how they could possibly know whether or not it complied with their oaths to protect the Constitution. This question led me into a review of the government's history, and a careful reexamination of the provisions of the National Constitution.

While the Congress growled over the passage of the health care bill, I began to dig and learn. I discovered the mismanagement of the Constitution and the trampling of self-government that we as Americans had allowed, especially in the last 100 years. The American public had failed to demand that Congress enforce the power of the Constitution, and without requiring that the Constitution be strictly followed, or changed, the power of the federal government was permitted to grow without limits.

The society of the twentieth century was far different, indeed, from the society that founded the Constitution, and its needs were vastly different. Remarkably, the founders recognized the natural evolution of societies, and they provided a means for changing the Constitution according to the evolving requirements of society, but this provision often has been ignored. Instead, common citizens permitted their representatives to work around the Constitution by allowing the Supreme Court to read new meaning into its words. The dangerous result is that the power of the contract was lost, and the power of the government was transferred from the people to a central few.

As power was negligently surrendered to federal leaders, I realized a centralized authority took shape with its own ideas of civic rights and debt management. The idea of using federal authority to provide human resource assistance was developed around the premises of progressives, socialists, and communists. Unchecked federal growth left the nation with an extraordinary list of failures, beginning with the accumulation of an unmanageable, and unrestrained, national debt. The major cause of debt for much of the nation's history has been wars, commonly it more than doubles after every national conflict. The debt has grown more rapidly over the last eighty years, however, as the result of human resources spending. Today, the biggest budget expenditure is for human resource handouts. The most troubling aspect is that America borrows from other countries in order to provide much of these benefits.

Unlimited human resource spending not only is the major cause of the enormous US debt, but also it may be the single greatest source of division among the American people. The split between US citizens is likely caused because the plain language of the Constitution does not authorize human resource spending. Public assistance spending grew out of creative interpretation around the principles of the Constitution in order to build the growing menu of human resource programs. Wording of the Constitution is plain and simple, and it was meant to be. If Americans ever want to resolve their differences and control the spending on human resources, then the Constitution must be changed in order to explicitly provide for such programs, and limits must be placed upon the amount of authorized support. These provisions must be written into the national contract and accepted by the people, which will effectively take such programs out of the hands of the central government and return it to the people.

After reviewing the history of changes in government I just couldn't keep quiet. I was finally old enough to recognize the erosion of personal freedom that had occurred in my lifetime, and it was evident that federal control of citizens' personal choices would continue to grow. As a result, I decided to write down what I had learned. My notes became a book that was published in 2012 called, *Malfeasance In Office*. It is a modest study of the Constitution and a review of the remarkable list of failed government programs that have resulted from the nation's wandering from its contract.

A few chapters of *Malfeasance In Office* recall the sources of the principles of the Constitution and how the country has drifted from its provisions. The founders based it all upon human unalienable rights and self-government by public opinion. Today, the distinction between unalienable and statutory rights has been lost, and many Americans have forgotten, or never knew, the difference, and so they have allowed themselves to be manipulated into more government controls by wily government officials.

The list of failed programs that are discussed is quite long. It begins with the billowing debt that started at $75 million in 1791, until it has reached $16 trillion. Other infamous government programs include the creation of wholly owned government corporations such as the mortgage giants, Fannie Mae and Freddie Mac, AMTRAK, and the US Postal Service. Other historical government failures include subsidies, immigration control, and misplaced spending on education.

Perhaps the largest perversion of American freedom originates in the progressive income tax system that was adopted in 1913. The history of this repulsive tax system is summarized with an inside look at how it works and its terrible waste. The roots of the idea of progressive taxes can be traced to the early communist movements outlined by Karl Marx in the nineteenth century. Now, the system is used as much to support social programs, as it is to raise operating revenue. Cost of social programs, such as earned income credit, are buried in the operation of the tax code, and now the health care act not only adds to the administrative costs of the tax code, but also uses the provisions of the tax system to impose personal penalties as justification to force Americans to participate.

The consequence of unrestrained human resource spending is severe strain on the federal budget. The national budget is analyzed in a chapter of *Malfeasance In Office*, with some surprising conclusions. A discussion of the principles of budgeting begins with the construction of a business budget, followed by analysis of the problems business managers face when trying to keep within budget margins. The business examples, then, are compared to the fiscal estimates for the 2010 national budget. The major sources of annual budget overruns are revealing. It's astonishing that payouts for human resource spending are about two-thirds of the entire amount spent by the federal government.

Closing chapters of *Malfeasance In Office* include the call for revolution, a civil revolution, to reestablish constitutional supremacy, to correct missteps of the past, and to adopt constitutional revisions to meet the needs of modern society. Some of the proposals to restore civil authority may appear extreme at first hand, and perhaps they are, but surprisingly, many of the suggestions are not new at all, but were proposed by the brilliant constitutional minds that created the foundation for our government today.

With the rollout of *Malfeasance In Office*, there was a need for some sort of basic marketing plan. A short brochure called, "Did You Know?" was created to introduce the book release. It was a series of thoughts that are not often considered by people during the routine of their daily lives. Details of each question, or tease, are included in this edition of *The Core Question*, and they include subjects such as the true American Dream and the cause of America's sharp division today. The four major breaches of American freedom are briefly reviewed, and the explosion of unearned human resource benefits are explained and laid bare for consideration. One of the most important parts of the Constitution that is reviewed is its unique safety valve. Unfortunately, a majority of Americans appear to be unaware of this safeguard the founders put in the Constitution for us; it is the ultimate protection of our individual liberty.

In the end there turned out to be twelve notes in "Did You Know?" These summary notes seemed like a fitting introduction to the essays in *The Core Question*, and so they have been included for that purpose.

After publication of *Malfeasance In Office*, it was decided to develop individual additions and details of its various subjects for the Internet. It started slowly with my pet peeve, the progressive income tax system, and then snowballed into subject after subject. Eventually, it was decided to set up each individual piece in the format of an essay. Not by design, a dozen of these essays were the result intended for Internet promotion of the original book.

When the group of essays was finished, it was noticed that a fairly substantial body of work was the result; and, after considering it further, it looked like the collection would make a fitting companion piece to go with *Malfeasance In Office*. And so *The Core Question* was born, with the idea that each book complements the other. *Malfeasance* covers more subjects in more depth, while *The Core Question* is composed of short, individual discussions in a more conversational tone. The collection of essays includes both instruction and ideas for reflection by the reader. None of the essays are comprehensive treatments, but are short arguments intended to kindle the interest and thought of the reader. Similarly, none are intended as conclusive answers.

The twelve essays can be read in any order; each stands alone, but the order of arrangement in the book sets up the first four to establish basic concepts and definitions that may be found in the remaining eight. The first four focus on the basis of the Constitution to make a starting foundation for youthful readers and those who may be less informed about the Constitution's beginning, or maybe would like a short refresher. There is a description of America's turn away from the republican form of government that has been developing for a century or more, and the warning from the founders that our self-government could be lost in a generation if not carefully guarded. The elementary theory of our government is reviewed in these essays and the probable answer to the reason for the great rift that exists between Americans is explained by the theories of early government philosophers. The fourth article wraps up the spotlight on the Constitution with a reminder of the responsibilities of each US citizen, and the four duties that each of us should be committed to fulfilling as responsible countrymen.

Specific issues are the theme of the last eight essays. They include background and discussion on everyday American complaints on subjects such as taxes, budget debt, human resource spending, excessive power in the executive and supreme court branches, career politicians, and government jobs and unions. It is suggested that changes in the operating structure of these activities are central to the preservation of the Constitution and adapting it to modern society.

Each essay is more or less set up in a format of five elements. There is an introduction section that describes the situation to be discussed. This is followed with a short statement of the core question, and thus the title of the entire collection. Background on the subject is given with a short history and a description of the evolution to the present day situation. Individual points of discussion follow the historical section with various facts and opinions on the subject, and then each essay is wrapped up in the conclusion with ideas for change to be considered.

In support of the frequent references to parts of the Constitution it was decided to include a copy of it for cross study. Readers are encouraged to read this concise, plain, and specific National Law, and to decide for themselves what it says. Where our government has strayed beyond its framework, individual citizens must insist on the return to its principles, and on clear changes where needed.

As indicated earlier, none of this is expected as final solutions to the problems of modern American society. Its purpose is to resurrect and reconsider the masters' ideas of freedom, and to learn again the true idea of self-government. Perhaps readers can begin thinking of new ways to break apart from the constant current dialog that is fed to us by political party lines and slick campaign managers. Perhaps it is time to reverse some of the misdirection of the last fifty or one hundred years. Perhaps now is the time to let the voices of contributing Americans be heard, as opposed to the voices of special interest groups and noncontributing Americans. Let us learn and accept our responsibilities of citizenship to save the true Dream before the last lamp is extinguished.

Frank E Cahill
2014

Did you know?
A Prologue

OUR TRUE DREAM

The opportunity to work and prosper in the US is merely a by-product of the true American Dream. The true dream of our forefathers, and our dream for our children, is the legacy of our natural right to govern ourselves, and not to be governed by a central authority. Every free American must support the Dream by fulfilling four essential duties of citizenship; these are jury duty, voting, contributing to the necessities of the government, and guarding the activities of government representatives. The founders of freedom intended that the people make the laws, not a small group of individuals attempting to set uniform rules for all.

BLURRED AMERICAN RIGHTS

Many Americans, and their government representatives, are confused about their guaranteed constitutional rights. The distinction between unalienable and statutory rights is obscure or altogether lost. Guaranteed constitutional rights are unalienable rights; these are the natural birthrights of all human beings to free conscience, belief, and activity. Unalienable rights can never be morally revoked, and when mankind restricts them it is a corruption against nature. Statutory rights are privileges granted by government regulations, and may be changed at the will of lawmakers. Welfare, food stamps, and other human resource programs are examples of vested statutory rights. Health care insurance is often presented as the right of every American; however, it is a statutory right that can be withdrawn, not an unalienable gift of nature. It is an important difference. Health care and social welfare are not guaranteed by the Constitution.

PROTECTED BY THE JURY SYSTEM

The US is one of the last countries to use the jury system. James Madison was the father of the Constitution who submitted a draft that was based upon the idea of self-government through public opinion to be implemented using the common law jury system. The whole idea of the common law jury was to protect the people's rights against overzealous or corrupt officials. The common-law jury decided both facts AND LAW during the first one hundred years of US history, until the Supreme Court bound juries to the instructions of the court, and restricted them to deciding only the facts of each case.

THE MAIN CAUSE OF A DIVIDED AMERICA

James Madison and the other founders were part of great discussions often called the Era of Enlightenment. Madison was influenced by the ideas of David Hume, the renowned Scottish philosopher, who observed that the greatest cause of factions is centralized government. Undoubtedly, this is the root of the tremendous fracture in America today. As the federal government assumes control of most American activities, groups with common interests are formed to influence the centralized government to govern according to their choices. Competing coalitions develop in the effort to gain control of the entire country, and so America is split. When self-government is restored to the people at the state and local levels, where they know what is best for their individual communities, then the nation will likely heal from the constant strife of groups trying to control the whole country.

A NEW FEDERAL PURPOSE

The founders' vision of a federal government was based upon three needs: provide for defense, insure fair trade and commerce, and maintain courts for fair and equal laws. Today's modern government has adopted a fourth purpose, social insurance. Search as one will, there is really nothing in the Constitution, nor in the writings of the founders, that establishes a commitment for human resources. Most early Americans didn't view providing human resource benefits as a responsibility of the federal government. The need to support others is a development of twentieth century constitutional interpretation. Social programs crept into the government through clever weaving of larger meaning into the simple wording of three clauses of the Constitution. By claiming to have unlimited (implied) power to make social laws (regulate commerce) on a national scale (general welfare), the federal government has expanded its reach into human resource laws.

FOUR LARGE BREACHES OF FREEDOM

There have been three major changes in the last one hundred years that have steered us away from the true American Dream and toward a centralized government that strip away the natural right to self-govern. It began with the progressive income tax system. Social Security was second, in 1935, and Medicare followed in 1965. These two tax schemes have drained national assets through the action of forcing the younger generation to accept the debts of their fathers. All of America's founders would have objected to this immoral plan. Unless a change can be made, there will be a fourth millstone in the transition to centralized planning; of course, this is the universal health care mandate. Curiously, through the decision by the Supreme Court (it's a tax), it further demonstrates the abuse of the progressive tax system to force people to comply with the dictates of the central city.

BIGGEST LOSS OF PERSONAL FREEDOM

The founding fathers were against a progressive income tax system. The system of today remained unconstitutional until ratification of the Sixteenth Amendment in 1913; there were no provisions for tax withholding until 1942. The framers of the Constitution avoided a direct tax, and the original provisions of the national contract stated no direct tax could be imposed unless it was proportioned equally for all citizens (somewhat like the flat tax ideas). When the Congress tried to establish the progressive system, the Supreme Court struck it down until the Constitution was changed. The country's revenue for the first one hundred years was largely drawn from tariffs and excise taxes (similar to the fair tax ideas).

COMMUNIST PROGRESSIVE TAX

The *Communist Manifesto* lists "Ten Steps to Communism." Step number two is to implement a heavy progressive income tax. When this abusive system was implemented in the US, it became the biggest breach of American freedom, the beginning of class warfare, and the start of a one-hundred-year transition to a centralized government. A governing class has developed that uses the progressive income tax system to control the behavior of citizens, instead of using taxes as the ways and means to raise revenue for the nation's business.

DICTATORSHIP BY EXECUTIVE ORDERS

The transitions of the twentieth century include misuse of the presidential power of executive orders. Originally intended as an administrative tool for coordinating the activity of the president's staff, it has grown until the Executive Branch writes laws in place of the Congress. Worse, czars who are not elected by the people, not confirmed by the Congress, and who may also enforce their own rules without the consent of the Congress, often are the authors of executive orders today. It's rule of boards instead of rule of people. The idea gained force when Theodore Roosevelt decided that if the Constitution didn't specifically prevent an action, then he could use the executive order to move the country in a progressive direction for the good of the people. The uses of executive orders exploded until it has become a mild form of dictatorship, and it is not inconceivable that its misuse could result with total control by one individual or department.

HUGE COST OF UNEARNED BENEFITS

The cost of Medicaid, food stamps, Supplemental Security Income (SSI), and numerous other free programs cost the country nearly as much as Social Security and Medicare. Although Social Security and Medicare are troubled programs, most recipients have paid in to the plan, and continue to pay part of their premiums. Conversely, individuals who have paid nothing into the treasury draw from the free programs. Today, the cost of unearned payouts nearly matches the amount of earned payouts.

FEDERAL BENEFITS FOR POLITICIANS

Career politicians were not federal employees until about 1946. A few years earlier they attempted to include themselves as federal employees, but there were strenuous objections by Americans. Nevertheless, they slithered and manipulated their way to becoming part of a system that provides extraordinary pay and benefits in comparison to the average working Americans that they are supposed to represent.

OUR UNUSED SAFETY VALVE

The genius of the American founders left an active Constitution with a unique safety net that has never been used. It's found in

Article Five. In the event of an unresponsive government, the self-governing people may reclaim their right by calling for a Constitutional Convention. On the application of two-thirds of the States a convention may be called for proposing amendments, and when ratified by three-fourths of the States, the amendments shall become law. This could become the people's revolution to repeal the Sixteenth Amendment and to clarify the meaning of the "general welfare," "commerce," and "implied powers" Clauses. If the country is to provide for human resources, such as welfare and Social Security, then this should be specifically written into the Constitution, WITH LIMITS on how much. This could be the way to require a balanced budget amendment, and to limit the percentage of the country's output that can be taken from the people by taxes. It might be the only way to eliminate the abuse of Executive Orders, and to impose term limits on Congress, and possibly Supreme Court Justices. And once and for all, members of Congress could be removed from the rolls as federal employees.

Ideas of Freedom
The Basis of the Constitution

THAT A NEW CONSTITUTION IS NEEDED was the predominate belief of American leaders in the years after the country won its independence. The Articles of Confederation simply weren't working, because the federal government was powerless to collect taxes, and the bills left by the Revolutionary War were piling up. George Washington and colleagues feared the country could collapse.

James Madison was a strong supporter for a new start with a new contract, so he and others initiated efforts for a new Constitutional Convention in 1787. He accepted the task, with fellow delegates, of developing a draft, and made an outline for a new national contract called the Virginia Plan. It set the agenda for debate on the idea of population-weighted representation in congress. Madison and others were well prepared for the task as a result of years of study and experience. The world was alive with political theories at that time as ideas of freedom and human rights were evolving. The ancient principles of human rights established by Israelite and Anglo-Saxon governments were the starting point, and the example the British Parliament set for including the voice of the people in government was additional inspiration for self-government. Political philosophers around the world were exchanging and debating theories on types of governments, how they should function, and their role in the lives of people.

Thomas Jefferson was in the middle of it; government was one of his passions and he had spent years reading both ancient and modern theories of government. He had learned a great deal from personal experience, too. During his service to Virginia he spent several years reviewing the Virginia Constitution resulting with his recommendations for over a hundred changes. Jefferson had company, though. John Adams was a similar student of government, and he wrote the best part of the Massachusetts Constitution. Other experienced constitutional specialists were John Rutledge, Oliver Ellsworth, and James Wilson, all who were experienced avid students of government.

Using Madison's outline and others, the state delegates debated and exchanged ideas for two months. Anxious to return to business at home, the delegates appointed a special committee to compile the notes taken during the Convention's debates, with the provisions of the Virginia Plan, and with the existing Articles of Confederation, to develop the first draft of a new Constitution. The new draft was reviewed and molded into the document presented for ratification. Approval didn't come quickly, though; the states were reticent, somewhat mistrustful, so there was considerable opposition to the new Constitution. The deciding factor became a promise by George Washington to meet their wishes for a Bill of Rights as soon as an approved Constitution placed the new government in operation. Honoring Washington's promise, James Madison authored twelve amendments to the Constitution, but only ten were ratified, until 1992 when the eleventh of his proposals became the Twenty-seventh Amendment.

While the story of the founders' work is fascinating, the sources of the provisions that they incorporated into the Constitution are essential to a deeper understanding of the mutual contract that Americans share today. Their studies resulted in the brilliant provisions to utilize public opinion to honor the natural right to self-govern, and their decision to ground the Constitution on common law to protect the rights of the individual remains the corner stone of American freedom today. Of course they decided on a democratic republic as the most efficient transfer of lawmaking power, but the founders thought it was critical to protect the rights of the minority as well as respect the will of the majority. Finally, with ingenious foresight, the convention wrapped the whole document with a flexibility to both adapt to the needs of future generations and to protect their freedom from the threat of an ever-growing government.

The story is captivating. The sources of ideas may be surprising. The final theory behind the Constitution, and what it means may be unexpected.

THE CORE QUESTION is whether Americans properly understand the US Constitution and do their part to protect its unique provisions for their common security?

THE INFLUENTIAL IDEAS THAT SHAPED the US Constitution

were the combination of ancient theories, ideas of world philosophers during the cultural period of educational enlightenment, and the dreams of American political theoreticians. Histories of ancient governments included the Israelites, Anglo-Saxons, Greeks, and Romans. As a student, Thomas Jefferson noticed the recurring theme of sacred rights in the ancient writings. They began with the idea that each human has natural rights at birth, which are really no different than the rights of any living creature of nature. Human rights were the fundamental law of nature that all people are born with the right to their thoughts, the right to their conscience, and the right to live their life in their own way. These original rights were called unalienable rights in the eighteenth century, which simply meant that these are gifts of nature that cannot be revoked or seized. In contrast, there was the concept of vested rights, or rights granted by government statutes. These would be protections of laws, for example, that could be changed by the government.

The ultimate idea of unalienable rights was that no government, office, or agency has a right to exist without the consent of the people, and it is forever the right of the people to control government, and to withdraw its right to exist if determined by their wish.

Around the sixteenth century the ancient ideas were more or less rediscovered by thinkers and academics. It was the beginning of an explosion of ideas in science, economics, the humans condition, and of course, politics. By the time the Continental Congress was convened, there was a multitude of ideas already written, and more being rapidly added during their lifetimes. Many American leaders were participants, too, and they included many of the ideas, both new and old, into the constitutional framework.

The founders knew they wanted a government controlled by the people. Thomas Hobbes, an English theorist, stated there were only three types of self-government: democracy, communism, and centralized democracy. He said these were the purest definitions, and all other self-ruling governments were variants of these three. In his descriptions of government by the people, Hobbes observed that a democracy without protections could be just as oppressive as any form of government. He warned that hundreds of tyrants could be as repressive as one. Protection of the minority was an important part of freedom for all.

John Locke, another English academic, has been called the father of classic liberalism, which at that time meant those in favor of limited government and individual liberty. Around 1690 he wrote that any group of people can surrender certain natural freedoms in exchange for security and the order of society, and he emphasized the people's right to withdraw what they may surrender. Locke's ideas heavily influenced the opinions of Jefferson and Madison, and Alexander Hamilton. As a result, Thomas Jefferson drew heavily on Locke's ideas and words when he authored the Declaration of Independence.

Several Scottish thinkers contributed to the enlightenment, and James Wilson, one of the committee members that were selected to draft the Constitution, was a Scottish emigrant that studied the Scottish enlightenment before he left Scotland to settle in Pennsylvania. Two of his mentors were David Hume and Adam Smith. Not only were they heavy influences on Wilson, but also Madison and the other founders. Hume, in particular, observed the factions between people in society. He concluded that factions are the nature of man existing everywhere in degree according to circumstances. Hume thought the most common cause of factions was the unequal distribution of property, and he further concluded that centralized government magnifies factions among people. How to handle factions was a key problem for James Madison when he was working on the initial design of the Constitution. Adam Smith, on the other hand, was regarded for his views of economics and proper government expenses; in fact, he is called the father of economics in response to his composition of the *Wealth of Nations*. It was Smith's belief that legitimate government expenses were limited to national defense, insuring fair contracts, establishing a justice system, banking regulation, and building infrastructure. A great deal of Smith's ideas of government was used to limit the purpose of government when the Constitution was formed.

The last group of ideas outside the colonies came from the French thinkers. Their names were long, or they used pen names, and so they were often referred to by a single name, such as Rousseau, Condorcet, Montesquieu, and Voltaire. The French added to the idea that public opinion should be the absolute political authority and is the basis of a stable government. Madison latched on to this idea and structured the provisions of the Constitution to support this idea.

Rousseau wrote, around 1762, his agreement that man is born free, but is chained in the world because one individual thinks himself master of others. He was technically from Geneva, a city-state in those days, and so he believed a republic government could only work on a small scale. Larger sized countries would be too big for efficient communication and agreement, and simply could not function properly as a republic. He thought, for example, that a republic would work fine in Geneva, but in a country as large as France, it would fail. This was a dilemma for an architect such as Madison, because the United States was much larger than France, and it would be necessary to solve the problem of size.

Condorcet's idea of a Constitution founded on public opinion was illuminated by his contrast of public opinion versus popular opinion. He described popular opinion as a temporary sentiment of the people that is usually driven by the passions of immediate interests. If unchecked, popular opinion can develop into a sovereign rule of oppression; an example in modern times is the rise of the cruel Nazi regime. Public opinion on the other hand, is described as a composite of passion and reason. It develops in time through communication, reason, and conformity of sentiment. It is a simultaneous communication between government and people to shape the national conscience. Condorcet stressed that communication is essential for developing public opinion, and that governments should not relent to short-term popular ideas, but follow the informed public.

Perhaps the greatest French influence came from Baron de Montesquieu. Among his ideas of government was the separation of powers. He divided national authority into two types: administrative and sovereign. A free people are the sovereign power, and the administrative authority is delegated to executive, legislative, and judicial elements of government. Building upon the checks and balances used by the Romans, his description of separation of powers into three branches was a fresh threat to the long-established feudal system in Europe. Naturally the founding fathers admired this system and combined it with their admiration of the British Parliament with its people's house that was granted a voice in their government.

The US had dozens of freedom thinkers, too, and many had direct experience with writing constitutions from scratch for their state governments. They had already learned many lessons about what works, and what is not so good. To mention a few is to leave out many, but there were notable contributions. The Adams cousins were deeply involved with the independence effort from the beginning. Samuel Adams was a fiery defender of freedom as the unalienable gift of the Creator. John and Samuel joined James Bowdoin in drafting the Massachusetts Constitution about ten years before the US convention, and John Adams believed the Congress should be a miniature of the makeup of the country.

Thomas Jefferson, James Madison, and Edmund Randolph were terrific constitutional minds from Virginia. About the same time Adams was working on the Massachusetts Constitution, Jefferson was given the task of studying and revising the State laws of his home state, and he drafted 126 bills in three years to streamline the government. In his studies of government he concluded that there are only two ideas of government. One system fears and distrusts the people and takes all power to a higher elite class for sensible administration. The alternative way has confidence in the people as the most honest and safe method to preserve freedom. Jefferson feared the growth of government and warned that a group of elitists are as oppressive as a single dictator. James Madison was Jefferson's protégé. Madison was a sharp student and worked with Jefferson on the Virginia Statute for Religious Freedom to separate church authority from government. When Jefferson was in Europe he literally sent crates of books about various forms of government theory to Madison at home. Madison poured over the information in a fruitful and scholarly research. He studied the problems of each and began to formulate solutions that would find their way into the US version to come.

The committee assigned to the job of submitting the first draft of a new Constitution was called the Committee of Detail, and the five men that formed it were brilliant students of government theory. John Rutledge from South Carolina became the second Chief Justice of the US Supreme Court. Edmund Randolph of Virginia was the country's first Attorney General. Nathaniel Gorham from Massachusetts had served for a time as the president of the Continental Congress during its critical days. Connecticut's Oliver Ellsworth was chosen to follow John Rutledge in protecting the new Constitution as the third Chief Justice of the Supreme Court. James Wilson, the Scotland transfer, was perhaps the most brilliant constitutionalist of them all, and also served on the Supreme Court.

Dozens more dedicated citizens added their thoughts and ideas to the debate and construction of the Constitution. With the help of ancient principles combined with the great minds of Europe and America, the Constitution was no accident.

PUTTING IT ALL TOGETHER was the mammoth assignment that James Madison accepted when he began outlining a Constitution. He would put together a plan of six core elements of the US Constitution.

The Constitutional Convention would take place without the presence of either Thomas Jefferson or John Adams. Both were serving as foreign ministers at the time. Jefferson was in Paris, and Adams assigned in London. Nevertheless, Madison and the other delegates were prepared and up to the task.

Madison was one of the first delegates to arrive at the convention site, so while he waited he began work on the outline. The rest of Virginia's delegation soon followed to work with Madison on his outline. The final product leaned heavily on the concepts of Locke and Montesquieu, and it was submitted to the convention as the Virginia Plan.

Most of the delegates to the convention already knew what they wanted from the new government, so Madison organized it. The outline called for a federal government with limited purpose. It would be governed by the people through public opinion formed by strong ties of communication between the federal offices and the people. The entire system would be built upon common laws and juries to protect the rights of the individual. By balancing federal powers it would be possible for each state to govern itself as a small republic, relying solely on the federal government for the protections and safeguards of the whole. By limiting federal power, the problem of factions could be minimized by letting each area of the country, or state, tailor their rules to their specific needs and style of life. The use of two legislative houses and the checks and balances of the executive and judicial branches would further protect the rights of the minority segment of society. The last element included an innovative provision to allow the Constitution to remain in the hands of the people and to change with the needs of society.

The Constitutional Convention began by reviewing not only the

Virginia Plan, but also the Articles of Confederation, and the Pinckney Plan submitted by Charles Pinckney. Debate progressed as the delegates considered each point of the proposals.

The creators of the Constitution decided the most effective way to protect the natural rights of citizens was by limiting the authority of the federal government. This led them to restricting its purpose to preventing the threat of foreign force, and limiting fraud, monopoly, and public indecency. It was a simple and straightforward purpose that ultimately resulted in twenty specific powers of government. It was their intent that the federal government should be contained within the boundaries of these provisions.

The twenty powers of government were established to provide for a common defense, fair trade and commerce, and a court system for fair and equitable laws, nothing more. The federal government was authorized to lay and collect taxes, raise a military force, establish rules for citizenship, maintain communication, and manage federal lands. Many of the states, especially the smaller ones, remained suspicious of a federation. Their individual choices and lifestyles were dear to them, and they didn't want a group of individuals from North to South to tell them how to live. The limited power of government was an important step to soothe this concern.

Virtually all of the delegates accepted Condorcet's belief that government should change with the ideals of society by updating itself according to mature public opinion. This would be structured into two legislative houses, the election of a president by the people, and the confirmation of court justices by the senate.

Eighteenth century Americans admired the common law ideas of the English Magna Carta of 1215. It established the difference between civil law and common law. Based upon law precedent established by the people, common law was based upon case law. It adopted the idea that it is unfair to treat similar facts differently at different times, and so a body of precedent becomes common law. Conversely, civil laws are adopted through legislation and established by government officials. Building upon this idea, the founders wrote guarantees for individual rights to trial by jury into the Constitution. In its earliest form, a common law jury served in courts, and they decided both facts and law. In other words, if the jury disagreed with the explanation of law by the judge or attorneys, it could rule in favor of the defendant, thus deciding the law in the case. It wasn't lawful for the jury to harm the defendant, but it could determine favorably in the case. Thus, the common law jury was the ultimate protection of the individual from the government. The system of the common law jury remained in effect until 1895. Today the jury is limited to finding the facts of a case, rather than both facts and law. The US government is one of the few in the world with guarantees for a trial by jury.

Strong communication would be a chief requirement for the success of a republic. Remembering Rousseau's suggestion that republics can work only on a small scale, the founders included provisions for efficient roads and postal service. These were the primary means of communication at the time. It may be one of the reasons the postal service was included in the Constitution, and was one of the first four positions in President Washington's Cabinet. The refinement of communication was a second reason for limiting federal power over the states. Each state would be a small republic that could adequately communicate through newspapers, roads, and mail with federal business.

Protecting the minority from the majority, of course, was built upon Montesquieu's theory of three divisions of equal power in the federal government between executive, legislative, and judicial branches, and a division of the legislative branch into two houses. The idea of two houses became a central sticking point for the smaller states until the idea arrived to provide equal representation in the Senate. Later, while waiting for ratification of the Constitution, James Madison would describe in the *Federalist* the idea of the balance of powers. He wrote, "The House of Representatives is a national body, not a federal representation, that derives its powers from the people in the same proportion as they are in their state. The Senate receives coequal power of each state such that it is a federal body rather than national. The executive branch is a mixture of national power, determined by electoral votes, from the proportional representation in the House and coequal power in the Senate. Thus the government was intended to be of balanced and mixed character."

Last, but probably most important, was the provision for a flexible and changeable Constitution with a unique safety valve for the people. How far sighted they were to recognize that society and civilization would continue to evolve and change from what it was during their lives. Even more wonderful were their thoughts for future American generations in a plan that could continue to support new ideas. This was the genius of the provision of changes to constitutional law through amendments. It allows the people to lawfully agree to change the Constitution by amendment in cases where government action does not conform to constitutional rules.

Perhaps the most ingenious protection, though, occurs in Article Five of the Constitution. The founders left a safety outlet, a way out for a people dealing with an unresponsive government. Article Five of the Constitution allows the States, on the application of two-thirds of State Legislatures, to call a convention for proposing amendments. Amendments put forth in this method may be ratified just like any other amendment, following approval of three-fourths of the States. The ultimate power remains in the hands of the people to set the direction of government through the Constitution.

Edmund Randolph summarized the genius of the Constitution in his preface to the draft of the Constitution submitted to the convention. He said they decided to use simple and precise language, and general propositions, such that the Constitution could be accommodated to times and events.

RATIFICATION WAS SLOW. Work on ratification continued about two years. James Madison, Alexander Hamilton, and John Jay, the first Chief Justice of the Supreme Court, worked diligently to explain the intent imagined when they were working on the new Constitution. They wrote a series of essays that today are a collection published as the *Federalist*. Some of the state delegates wanted a bill of rights before they left the convention, and it continued to be a strong sticking point for some. Ultimately, it took the incomparable trust in George Washington to swing the difference. He promised that after ratification each state could submit proposed constitutional changes to the first Congress. Their consummate trust in his character swung the deal, and James Madison was assigned the task of resolving some 189 suggested amendments. He was able to combine them into seventeen amendments, which were eventually reduced to ten and ratified. This is the all important Bill of Rights Americans turn to daily for their individual protection. Enough states accepted the Constitution in 1789 to form the Union, and Rhode Island was the last hold out until 1790.

CITIZENS TODAY CAN CONCLUDE that they have inherited the right to govern themselves through the goodness of the country's public opinion and its respect for the rights of others. Their rights are grounded on the principles of the common law jury. Each American should jealously guard this right and enthusiastically support it with their service when called to jury duty. It's a call that is not less important than military service.

The mutual contract is not dead or outdated. From the first day of ratification, it was meant to be changed according to the needs of the times, and the earliest citizens started it off with ten changes. It is the supreme law and must be followed to the letter, or changed if it doesn't work for what society needs. Every American should guard against allowing constitutional interpretations, instead of constitutional amendments that are discussed by the people and approved in the open. Too much interpretation of the Constitution by an elite few, in order to move society in a direction they believe is best, has left the country in a state of confusion and polarized factions. It's why some individuals conclude, or try to convince the uninformed, that the Constitution is obsolete. These comments are the direct result of a heavily centralized government that has developed through constitutional interpretation. President Washington warned against it. Our peculiar security is in the Constitution, and the worst offense to it and to us is to work around it or run over it.

In the end, it means a self-governing people must accept the responsibility for their government. It's a magnificent gift from the ingenious and selfless dedication of the men who framed the Constitution of the United States.

Saving the Constitution
A Case for Clarity

"WE HAVE TO PUT THIS RELIEF PACKAGE into law," the President pleaded.

"Yes, sir, but I think it stretches beyond the boundaries of the Constitution," the Chief Justice answered.

"You lawyers are good at working around contract law. Isn't there some way to squeeze a little extra meaning out of the Constitution? We really need this to support our campaign promises."

The Speaker of the House offered a little more incentive, "The polls show the people favor this relief project, and they're looking forward to it."

"Let us look at it, Mr. President," the Chief Justice agreed, "Like you said, there must be a way."

Of course this is a fictional conversation, but it may not be that far from reality, in view of the history of meandering around the Constitution by the Congress, the President, and the Supreme Court. It's interesting that evidently the popular majority of the country was in favor of their plan, but the plan was likely outside the limits established by the Constitution. Despite their self-described good intentions, there is a terrible threat to individual freedom by this kind of conduct from government officials or popular opinion.

The unique security of free people is established by the Constitution. It is a binding contract between citizens to control the powers they wish to surrender to a career government. It establishes a society of liberty in contrast to being a supervised society.

When the creators of the Constitution gathered to develop a new national charter, they were most concerned about what powers they were willing to relinquish to federal authority. When there were differences between the people and their federal employees, and the founders knew there would be, they wanted to provide peaceful remedies to protect the people from a war to regain lost rights. They did this with a simple agreement that is anchored by its Tenth Amendment. It speaks simply, "The powers not delegated to the United States by the Constitution, nor prohibited by it to the States, are reserved to the States, respectively, or to the people."

It begins with the concept of contract law. A contract is an agreement voluntarily entered into by two or more parties, each of whom intends to create legal obligations between them. When the provisions of the contract are contained within the framework of the written word, changes cannot be made without written changes to the contract. When there is a dispute over the meaning of the written contract, it could be arbitrated by a third party.

The US Constitution is the mutual contract among the American people to establish the powers of government they are willing to vest to federal authority. In exchange for safety and defense, rules of fair trade and commerce, and a system of fair courts, the writers granted twenty powers to the federal government. These powers are described by one sentence, albeit a long sentence, in Section 8 of Article I of the US Constitution.

Today, a fourth purpose, social insurance, has been added to the role of the federal government. Many citizens believe this has occurred outside the limits of the national contract and should not be allowed. Others think it is authorized indirectly between the lines. The ultimate arbiters, the national courts, have been less than consistent in their various constitutionality decisions concerning social insurance legislation, leaving the nation perplexed and divided.

American society has allowed the centralized culture in Washington to work around the Constitution. The responsibility for clarity lies with the people, or they will ultimately lose their authority. Today, the original twenty powers that limited the power of the federal government have expanded to limitless proportions. It is the handiwork of all three branches of government. The Executive Branch has used Executive Orders, rules from the Executive Office of the President, and agency laws from the Executive Cabinet to stretch the meaning of the Constitution. The Congress has perverted earmark spending, budget controls, and social spending beyond constitutional wording. The Supreme Court cooperated through policy-making interpretations and its activism.

Virtually all of the early leaders left writing that this could happen, and they guaranteed that it would happen if the people fail in their responsibility to insist on compliance with the Constitution or its change. Americans are divided today between a society of liberty that fiercely defends the original provisions and intent of the

Constitution, and a supervised society that seeks shelter in the judgment of federal agents.

The contrast of opinions focuses on five clauses of the Constitution and the Tenth Amendment. Those who have chosen to find larger meaning from the simple wording of the Constitution, in lieu of seeking open changes, have used the words of these five clauses to support their causes. These are clauses that are generally known as general welfare, regulate commerce, war powers, regulate federal lands, and implied powers. Through the art of creative inference the federal government has stretched its reach for all-consuming power. It will never stop growing until the people revolt. The originators of the Constitution left provisions within it to allow a peaceful reclamation of its authority. It will mean the people must unite to revise the Constitution to conform to the needs of society. Where the confusion over the meaning of the Constitution persists, then it should be clarified in the open, instead of behind the closed doors of the central city dealmakers. It will cause Americans to face the social issues of today, and then decide what society wants. If America has evolved into a society that wants more federal intervention into daily life, it should be defined and controlled. It's what the founders intended; the Constitution should support the changing needs of society.

The alternative could be dreadful. Without well-identified limits and control of the federal government, it will continue to pervert the Constitution to support its progress in becoming a totally centralized democracy. Agencies and boards will make all rules, and the people will be forced to comply. Choices will no longer be available.

THE CORE QUESTION is made up of two parts. What powers does the Constitution, and the people of the United States, confer on the federal government? Should the force of the Constitution be restored, or is government today what American society wants?

CONTROVERSY AROUND THE MEANING of the Constitution began immediately with the first administration regarding the Eighth Section of the First Article. Right away, the argument began with what powers does the Constitution (and the people of the Country) confer upon the federal government. It came to a head with Alexander Hamilton's proposal for a national bank. A bill to implement a national bank passed both the House of Representatives and the Senate and was submitted to President Washington for signature. President Washington was uncertain about the constitutionality of the bill, and so he asked James Madison for his opinion about it. Both Madison and Thomas Jefferson opposed the bill, because they thought it authorized bankers to issue money for the United States, which was outlined as a Congressional authority by the Constitution. But Alexander Hamilton sponsored the bill and urged the President to approve it. President Washington had tremendous admiration for Hamilton and his judgment. Hamilton served with President Washington during the Revolutionary War and distinguished himself as a courageous and excellent officer and soldier. He displayed outstanding heroism, and Washington relied upon him through several desperate engagements during the war. Also, Hamilton gained respect as one of the most successful businessmen in the United States.

The constitutionality debate focused on the First and Eighteenth Clauses of Article I, Section 8 of the Constitution. The First Clause includes the statement that the powers of Congress include the power to, "…provide for the common defense and general welfare of the United States; …" The Eighteenth Clause is the reputed "implied powers" clause that states that Congress may, "…make all laws which shall be necessary and proper for carrying into execution the foregoing powers…" President Washington trusted Alexander Hamilton with full confidence in his loyalty to the country and his understanding of finances. Because the country was strained with the heavy debts from the Revolutionary War, and because President Washington viewed the implementation of a national bank as a temporary measure, he accepted the idea of the implied powers of Congress described in Article I, Section 8, Clause 18 of the Constitution and signed the bill into law.

Thus began the idea of constitutional interpretation that has continued to this day, and the accompanying conflict of ideas of government's role in American lives. Alexander Hamilton believed government should control the people. He seemed to favor a government similar to Great Britain's where the welfare of the people was decided by the elites, which included the Monarch and the House of Lords established by heritage.

Both Hamilton and James Madison were tremendous supporters

of the Constitution through their explanatory *Federalist* essays written during the period of ratification of the new national contract. Both had similar views during this period, but Hamilton flipped his beliefs somewhat by the time he served in the first Cabinet. Alternatively, Madison explained that the twenty powers conferred in Article I.8 were meant to be the limit of power granted to Congress by the people. When the first Congress began to debate the meaning and intent of general welfare in the First Clause of Section 8, Madison told the members that if Congress can apply general welfare indefinitely, then it might take everything into its hands, including religion, education, schools, regulation of roads, and everything down to the minutest policy. Despite his warning, the government proceeded to progressively insert itself into all of these areas and more.

Following the first administration there have been debates and struggles around the meaning of the Constitution. It always reduces to one group that wants to remain true to the plain and simple text versus a group with new ideas it hopes to justify by reading abstract, or even new, meaning into the contract. The founders never would have opposed social changes if they were supported by the people and authorized by open changes to the Constitution, but they never would have agreed to working around it by small but powerful groups of individuals.

Gradually, the idea of a supervised American society has grown in the last one hundred years. Four huge steps began the interpretation revolution. These changes occurred roughly around 1913, 1936, 1965, and 2010. By 1913 American values apparently shifted to a socialist mindset. During this period, there was an enormous push toward social equality. It may have been fired by the relatively new Marxist theories and communism. Labor unions were forming to seek improved working conditions, and labor organizers seized the idea that the rich were using and oppressing the poor. A separate society of super rich industrialists didn't help, either. Rockefeller, Ford, Carnegie, Morgan, and others stepped into unimaginable wealth when they tapped the power of the industrial revolution.

Perhaps it was merely an era when Americans were sufficiently desperate and jealous enough to be susceptible to the class warfare that was used for the political aims of the dominant political parties and elected officials of the time. Nevertheless, the idea to soak the rich became a popular topic, and the concept of a progressive tax on different incomes at different rates was borrowed from communist doctrine. The progressive income tax system was ultimately implemented the right way. Congress first tried to use it without changing the Constitution, but the Supreme Court properly struck it down. There was just no creative way around the direct wording. Finally, the Congress asked the people to approve a change in the Constitution, and in 1913, the Sixteenth Amendment to the Constitution was ratified. Now the new tax system was legal, and properly approved.

This first step in a progressive movement to insert social programs into federal authority was followed by a massive program that was authorized by reading between the lines of the Constitution. This was when the Supreme Court upheld the Social Security Act in 1936. The Court finally settled the great disagreement over the meaning of the First Clause of the general powers section, which is to provide for the general welfare of the country. To be sure, the argument had continued for more than one hundred years since the first administration and the opposing constitutional interpretations of Alexander Hamilton and James Madison. Without question, Hamilton believed that any good cause for the country was within the power of Congress because this First Clause was a general grant of power to Congress. As previously reviewed, Madison felt this viewpoint would authorize Congress to delve into every area of individual lives. In 1936, the Supreme Court ruled that the First Clause of the general powers section is a separate and distinct power from the other nineteen listed in the section, and therefore, Congressional power is limited only by the requirement that its programs provide for the general welfare of the United States. Well, that was it. The door was officially opened to allow the federal government to set up infrastructure programs, social programs, national parks, and any federal program limited only by the imagination of the governing class. In rapid succession it was decided that building infrastructure was simply regulating commerce as provided in the Third Clause of general powers. Federal land banks were established under the interpretation that they fall under the authority of the war powers granted to Congress, such as in the Eleventh Clause of the general powers section; even though, the

Seventeenth Clause of this same section specifically restricts federal ownership of federal lands to the applications listed, and only with approval of the respective state.

A new generation of American society allowed the birth in 1965 of a similarly massive Medicare program. Elderly Americans were unable to purchase health care insurance, because their degenerative health and expenses were too much for the insurance industry. If citizens were unlucky enough to retire without a company health care plan, they were usually stranded with no health care insurance. So, the federal government decided to tap into the paycheck of working Americans again to pay for ambitious socialization of medical coverage. The program was disputed, but upheld under the similar provisions of the fair commerce and general welfare clauses.

Today, the current generation faces a comparable assault on the meaning of the Constitution by the fourth huge program to socialize America in the effort to provide health care insurance for everyone. It's the combination of the Health Care and Education Reconciliation Act and the Patient Protection and Affordable Care Act of 2010, more commonly just called the health care act. It left freedom loving Americans in disbelief that the federal government can force them to purchase health care insurance or pay a fine; and worse, that they will be required to report annually to the Internal Revenue Service that they are, or are not, properly insured. Of course, vigilant citizens were convinced that the bill was unconstitutional. Congress didn't know; in fact, some members didn't want to take the time to see what was in the bill in the first place, and urged fellow lawmakers to pass it right away and find out what is in it later. The First Congress likely would not have agreed with such a failure to support the Constitution.

The health care act was upheld by the Supreme Court, but not in the manner most people expected. Those who predicted it would be upheld thought the Court would turn again to the general welfare and commerce clauses. Surprisingly, it was upheld on the basis of the income tax rules, that is, the power to tax in Article I.8.1, and the progressive income tax law of the Sixteenth Amendment.

Regardless of individual beliefs on the social responsibility of society, the Constitution must be preserved in clear form and the power of the people secured. Today, this is not the case, and without this security, Americans are vulnerable to more rules set down by individuals, larger government agencies and expenses, and a final transfer of the power of a self-governing people to a centralized government. This means Americans must understand at least the controversial articles, then support necessary changes to secure the Constitution for the next generation.

THE ULTIMATE GUARANTEE IS PRESERVED in the Tenth Amendment of the Bill of Rights. It plainly states, "The powers not delegated to the United States by the Constitution, nor prohibited by it to the States, are reserved to the States, respectively, or to the people." It is intended to guarantee the clear division of authority between the federal government and states. Unfortunately, Supreme Court interpretations of other articles of the Constitution have dissolved the distinction between federal and state authority established by the Tenth Amendment. Today, the federal government directs the people concerning their schools, roads, housing, welfare, hospitals, banks, transportation, communication, air, water, land, and most everything else. It seems unlimited, because it is. Just as James Madison feared, Court interpretations of general welfare, commerce, and other provisions of the Constitution have left unlimited power in federal hands. It remains for the Tenth Amendment to guarantee that all powers not delegated to the United States remains with the people, but the government has claimed all powers in the name of the Constitution.

THE GENERAL WELFARE CLAUSE is first of the five clauses that have been constructed to allow the addition of social spending and other areas of government intervention. This is Article I, Section 8, Clause 1 of the Constitution. It gives Congress its power to collect taxes for various purposes including to, "…provide for the common defense and general welfare of the United States, …"

It is this clause that was the source of conflict between two ideas of its meaning since the earliest days of the Union. One group believes it limits Congressional authority to spend only for the twenty purposes established in Section 8 of Article I and that all spending must be for the good of all the Country, not just for individuals or special groups. The wording of this first article is the beginning of a sentence that runs continuously for the length of the entire Eighth Section; that is, it spans all eighteen clauses that establish

Congressional powers. It can be argued that this grammatical fact is further evidence that the purpose of the Eighth Section was to limit Congressional power to the elements specifically identified by it.

The contrasting view of the general welfare clause is that it grants Congress the power to make laws for any good cause beyond those listed by the eighteen clauses in Section 8. In other words, any idea for a law or rule that may be developed by the federal government is authorized by this clause of the Constitution, as long as the rule is for the good of all citizens and not preferential to any individuals or groups. Clearly, this results in limitless power as Madison observed.

In 1936 the Supreme Court endorsed the view of unlimited power. This decision effectively wiped out the foundation of a limited government bound by enumerated powers. Now, Congress has become the sole and supreme judge of the nation's general welfare, and it has established an agenda of vested social rights established by the federal government. Congressional leaders claim it is each citizen's right to have social insurance, retirement benefits, and health care. Unfortunately, though, many members of Congress do not make a distinction between statutory vested rights conferred by the government and unalienable human rights received at birth. Building on Social Security and Medicare, the Congress has used this interpretation to implement welfare, food stamps, and supplemental security income. It has grown to provide disaster relief, to regulate interstate roads, and to dictate uniformity of education throughout the country.

The unlimited social agenda has become the largest cause of uncontrolled spending by the government, and has led to the extraordinary debt that generations of benefit seekers have transferred to their children. Often termed entitlement spending, it has become difficult, if not impossible, for the government to plan for the demands of this type of spending. It has become firmly entrenched in American society, and turned out to be one of the biggest controls used by elected officials to secure their careers. As long as there are votes tied to handouts, a large number of citizens will support them.

THE COMMERCE CLAUSE is the Third Clause in Section 8 of Article I, and it has been one of the partners interpreted to extend federal power. This simple clause reads, "To regulate commerce with foreign nations, and among the several States, and with the Indian tribes." This clause identifies sovereign powers. Indian tribes at that time were not considered part of the US, and were treated similarly to the sovereignty of foreign governments. With regard to fair trade, the individual sovereignty of states was recognized, too. The whole purpose of this clause was to prevent states from making state laws to promote their local prosperity at the expense of the general welfare of the other states; in other words, to prevent gouging. In the eighteenth century, some states were deriving income for all state expenses from duties at entry ports. Even in contemporary times some states have attempted to claim unfair advantages of pipelines. The savvy pioneers of the Constitution knew such unfair practices would be economically repressive. Since one of the three purposes of government was to establish fair trade and commerce, this clause was included to grant Congress the power to control it.

The big question, though, has become what is commerce? As the federal government searched for ways to implement new restrictions on American life, it turned to digging into this clause as a way of justification. Various cases have found their way to the Supreme Court, and it ultimately ruled that commerce is every type of movement of persons or things, whether for profit or not. This came to include communications, transmission of intelligence, and the flow of services or power across state boundaries. It has even been ruled to include the negotiations that may involve future transportation.

This over reaching definition of commerce has led to federal control of railroads and interstate highways. It has erected dams as flood protection, then regulated navigation on resulting waterways and received payment for hydroelectric power generated. Federal over sight has dipped into labor relations, price regulations, interstate bus lines, and commodities. Virtually every facet of American life is viewed as commerce, and federal administrators have aggressively attempted to control it.

The conflict of views on the commerce clause is usually a split between those who believe the authority of the federal and state governments are mutually exclusive, and those who believe federal authority is fully complete and can impose regulations on any aspect of commerce. The federal government has used the second interpretation to build infrastructure and regulate its use.

CONGRESSIONAL POWERS ARE VESTED in Article I, Section 8, Clause 18. The controversy around this clause is whether it authorizes unlimited power to the Congress, or whether it specifically limits its power. This simple statement reads, "To make all laws which shall be necessary and proper for carrying into execution the foregoing powers, and for all other powers vested by this Constitution in the Government of the United States, or in any department or officer thereof." As the wordsmiths began to try to fit its meaning to support their agenda, various questions about it were discussed. Some focused on the meaning of the words, "necessary and proper," and as a result, the phrase is often referred to as the necessary and proper clause, the elastic clause, or the implied powers clause.

Those who believe the powers of Congress are limited by this clause usually point to the words, "for carrying into execution the foregoing powers." These people read the text plainly and literally, and so believe powers vested by this clause are limited to the twenty powers that are enumerated in Section 8, which includes the seventeen-clause description of the twenty powers and this eighteenth clause that provides their substance. Rather than a detailed description of each of the twenty powers, each power is generally described by a clause, and then Congress is authorized to add the detail by making necessary and proper laws to execute the functions of each of these clauses.

Conversely, others believe this is an elastic clause that provides unlimited and undefined power to the Congress, and that the Congress will be the judge of what is necessary and proper. By combining this interpretation with the broad treatments of the meaning of general welfare and commerce, unlimited power has been put into the hands of the federal government. It can do virtually anything that it determines is necessary and proper handling of the people, so long as it applies to everyone without special treatment of individuals and special groups.

REGULATION OF FEDERAL LANDS is authorized in Article I.8.17, and war powers are established in Article I.8.11. These articles work together to allow the federal government to own land in the US, but only with the permission of the legislature of the state where the land is located. Naturally, there is one exception, Washington,

DC, and this authority is similarly addressed in the Seventeenth Clause. The combined purpose of these clauses is to give Congress the authority to declare war; and, in support of national defense, the federal government may acquire state lands, "for the erection of forts, magazines, arsenals, dock-yards, and other needful buildings."

Today, however, the federal government owns state lands for reasons other than those listed. The situation evolved, more or less, as the country acquired new territories during its period of expansion. During the first expansion phases, the land in new states was sold to help pay the national debt, but the federal government stopped this practice when the Western territories were acquired. These lands have been permanently retained by the federal government, but not with the consent of the states, nor for purposes listed in the Seventeenth Clause. As a result, the federal government owns about thirty-five percent of America, and twelve western states each own less than seventy percent of their state land. The most extreme are in Nevada where the state owns less than thirteen percent, and Alaska, where the people of the state own only four percent of state land.

Instead of defense uses at the pleasure of the states, the federal government uses the land for national forests, parks, monuments, coal and oil reserves, land banks, land lease for profit, and wilderness areas with massive natural resources. By using the combinations of constitutional interpretation of the clauses for general welfare in Article I.8.1, regulating commerce, in Article I.8.3, necessary and proper laws in Article I.8.18, and the war powers and regulate lands clauses, the government may at any time take possession of any land for any purpose that it designates as necessary and proper for the general welfare of the country. Conceivably, the entire country could be owned by a federal government allowing citizens to live in it at the pleasure of the government; in contrast with, all land, water, and air being owned by citizens allowing the federal government to use it at the pleasure of the people.

UNLIMITED FEDERAL POWER IS A DISTURBING THOUGHT for a free people. It has crept into American society by manipulating the Constitution. The result is an expanding government that will never retract, never control itself, and never comply with the concept of a self-governing people. The founders intended for the Constitution to be changed in the open when the needs of society change, not to have the meaning squeezed and perverted by central authorities. George Washington wrote about it. Thomas Jefferson wrote about it. They warned their countrymen to never deviate from the Constitution. Change it if it is necessary, but never deviate from it.

The only answer to settle the differences of today is the proper answer intended by the founders, and that is to change the Constitution. James Madison believed that the way to prevent the government from overrunning its power was to change representatives. It is too late for that. The political monster that has grown from so many years of neglect would never allow such an adjustment. All branches, executive, legislative, and judicial, are in it together, and there are too many jobs and careers tied to current abuses. Alexander Hamilton believed if the federal government oversteps the boundaries of its authority, the people must return to the Constitution to correct the injury to their national contract.

Constitutional amendments are needed today to both settle the issues of the government's role in modern society, and to specify clear and exact limits of federal power. Declarative and restrictive amendments are needed to prevent misconstruction and abuse of the Constitution, ultimately to preserve it. If the American society of today favors a limited federal government, then it should be written into the contract. If American society of today favors a menu of social programs, then the power to do it should be written into the contract. If American society of today favors federal ownership of federal parks, it should be written into the contract. The people should decide in the open, not a central elite in the dark, what the role of the federal government should be, and then write it into the Constitution.

Four of the five clauses that have been discussed should be reviewed and revised by amendment to correct the federal government. The first and last clauses, that is, the general welfare and implied powers clauses, should be worded to specifically limit the powers of federal government to those specified by the Constitution. No open checkbook should be permitted. General welfare should be specifically limited to the enumerated powers, as should the necessary and proper powers that are disputed in the last clause.

Regulating commerce in the Third Clause needs to be tied down. It shouldn't be used to justify social programs, or health care, or any other abstract meaning that has been introduced in the last century.

Its meaning should be clearly tied to fair trade and commerce across state lines. All vagaries and abstractions should be eliminated.

Revision of the Seventeenth Clause is necessary, or the federal government should withdraw from state lands except for defense and proper purposes established in the war powers and federal lands clauses. Specific reasons for federal authority to hold land must be identified in order to protect the common citizens from its tyranny.

Obviously, if changes are made to tie government power to what the forefathers identified in the Constitution, then something has to give in today's society. Social Security, Medicare, welfare, disaster relief, national parks and monuments, and much more would not be covered by the Constitution. They would be out. That isn't the idea. It isn't what the founders intended, either. The founders were so brilliant in realizing that society and its needs will forever change. Thomas Jefferson thought a new Constitution for each generation would be in order.

In the world of today, if the American people, not the federal government, decide they want to spend a collective portion of their wealth on food stamps, natural disaster relief, and other social agendas, it is their right, and it should be specifically written into the Constitution. That is not to suggest an item-by-item authorization, but using the model of the founders, enough can be identified to limit its power. This way, if the federal government dreams up yet new programs to control private lives, it would be clearly unconstitutional, and the Congress must ask the people for an amendment if it wishes to enter unforeseen applications.

Some people claim the Constitution is an outdated document that is no longer applicable today. Either they don't understand the principle of change that is the heart of the Constitution, or they want to skirt around it, or abolish it, with the aim of increasing federal power or changing the American form of government altogether. Often it is same people who would like to see the United States join a world community or world government, which would make the US Constitution inapplicable. Instead, America would follow rules set by a world government.

Hybrid Society
The Transformation of America

THE CHANGES THAT OCCURRED in the last century were remarkable. From a carriage behind a team of horses to the comfort of a fast automobile guided by GPS; from a flimsy motorized kite that could fly around twelve miles an hour to flight near the speed of sound in better comfort than the horse and carriage; from investigation of the remote continents on Earth to exploration of the Moon; the changes are at once hard to believe and difficult to fully grasp. The changes brought by technology brought equally large changes in society and its ideas about the form and role of government. The government of the United States has not been exempt from the pressures of change. A result of the evolution of the US government is a hybrid society that is neither fully independent nor fully socialized. It has become, or is becoming, a welfare state that is well on its way to adopting the principles of a centralized democracy.

One hundred years of persistent change have transitioned American attitudes from a nation of independent, self-governing people to a nation of suffering dependents. Half the country views themselves as victims of society. They are the disabled, the underpaid, the unemployed, the single parent with a child out of wedlock, the poor and needy student, and the misfortunate masses begging for housing assistance, food stamps, and supplemental income. The transition of the attitude of Americans is an extraordinary change from the pride of self-assurance to no pride asking for a handout. The government has become mother to these people, and everyone wants to live at home.

This progressive evolution has had an extraordinary impact on the role the federal government has assumed. It is a completely different type of government from the one envisioned and established by the country's founders. Their goal was a small federal government designed to provide defense, fair commerce laws, and a court system. The great English philosopher, Thomas Hobbes, wrote that there are only three types of government: monarchy, aristocracy, and democracy. He thought all other systems were merely variations of these three. Various forms of democracies have been developed, including democratic republic, communism, and centralized democracy. America today is steadily transforming into a centralized democracy that will not reverse itself.

One of the interesting side effects of the conversion to central government is the development of a hybrid society. About half of the American population depends upon the government for some form of subsistence. The other half provides the cash. Both groups, unfortunately, are enslaved to the federal government. The dependent group is prohibited from improving their social status at the risk of losing their benefits, and the independent group must make annual reports and remit their support to the federal government for distribution to its captives.

Despite the assurances of the Constitution, the structure of the hybrid society violates the unalienable right to protect oneself from government control. When the working public is required to support the non-working public, then the federal government, and their dependents, regulates the individual conscience of productive workers.

In a centralized democracy the governing class is inspired to maintain and grow the role of government. It's how they hold their jobs, their livelihoods, and it gives them the distinction they seek. Their lives are filled with power and privilege, and their greed disconnects them from the people they are sworn to serve. Once entrenched in the throws of federal bureaucracy, the central planners believe only they know what is best for the people. Soon, citizens are totally governed by the rules of the central government, instead of the government following the rule of the people.

The hybrid society equals a divided nation. The rift between Americans has never been greater. The have-nots want what the haves enjoy, up to and including their lives. As the size of the dependent nation grows, the struggle will end with one victor, without consideration for the minority.

America will either reverse course or change forever. The country sags under the weight of a welfare system that consumes its productivity. Government continues to commit more support to public assistance than working Americans can produce. Unlimited rule by the central society is possible if it is allowed to continue. Salvation of the free people is only possible by a return to the provisions of the Constitution to restore civil authority in the country. The choice is between a democratic republic of self-rule, and a centralized democracy of bureaucratic rule. It cannot be mixed.

THE CORE QUESTION is whether Americans have lost control of the government, or whether the majority of citizens today favor a centralized federal government? Was this transition planned, or was it the result of an inattentive populous and government's misguided effort to help its citizens? There is evidence that it may be a combination of both. Where, then, should the transition to a centralized democracy stop, or can it be stopped at all? A more important question is whether ordinary Americans understand the basic difference enough to make a choice between a self-governed people and a society ruled by a small ruling class?

THE HISTORY OF THE TRANSFORMATION covers about one hundred years, more or less. There were fits and starts during the first half of the country's existence, but the major thrust of early national activity was to fiercely defend the Constitution and its guarantees.

The idea of freedom in America's earliest society was formed around the concept of unalienable rights. They viewed their personal rights as God given, which included freedom of their thoughts, of speech, and of conscience. The earliest Americans believed no government has the authority to limit personal rights, so they settled on the democratic republic that was established by the Constitution.

The founders of the Constitution originally intended for citizens to live in a free society. Their history included the flight of their ancestors from government tyranny. As a result, it was important to all of the states that the federal government should be limited in its role affecting daily life. They thought the union of the states should be to raise revenue for protection from foreign countries, to establish and maintain efficient communication, and for administration of the seat of government to establish equal rules of trade and commerce. Both their individual correspondence and the Constitution confirm that they wanted, and expected, little more from the federal government. It was never their intent that a small, elite group should make the laws and rule the country.

By the middle of the nineteenth century there were rumblings of upheaval among the European countries. Marx and Engels published their theories of communism, and the idea of the oppressed society was emphasized. This became a huge influence on the Russian revolution as it matched the cruelty of the mass revolution in France.

The turn of the twentieth century brought the era of the super rich in America, and the disparity between the rich and poor grew enormously. The unhappy life for workers in the United States became fodder for the political movement to involve government in solving their problems. The twentieth century, then, became the century of American transition to big government. The transformation of the last century has been fueled by four monumental changes. The first was the conversion to the progressive income tax that was implemented by the Sixteenth Amendment in 1913. A generation later, the massive Social Security program was enacted in 1935. Health insurance for the elderly was added to Social Security by the Medicare program in 1965, and huge welfare entitlements were written into law. The latest step in the centralization of American government occurred in 2010 when the Patient Protection and Affordable Care Act was approved. This would cement the idea of vested rights by claiming every citizen has a right to health care.

Only the first change of 1913 was done properly by amending the Constitution. This is the method of change the founders intended for societies that followed them. The ratification of the Sixteenth Amendment reflected the ideas of that generation and set the national mood for taking more from earners.

Social Security, Medicare, and welfare were the result of constitutional interpretation. The laws were passed and tremendous political power was brought to bear on their acceptance. Ultimately the addition of human resource spending was justified by imaginative evaluation of the commerce, general welfare, and implied powers clauses. The people were never asked openly to change the provisions of the Constitution to permit federal involvement in social issues. A new breed of self-interest legislators developed when career politicians realized that gifts to their voters would secure and insure long political careers and bloated pensions.

The Patient Protection and Affordable Care Act increased the intrusion into American private lives and strengthened the authority of the federal government to make its own laws above the purview of the people. It requires all Americans to obtain health care insurance or remit a penalty to the Internal Revenue Service. After referral to the US Supreme Court it was ruled constitutional as a tax penalty under the progressive income tax system.

These huge changes, and the constitutional interpretations that allowed them, have brought America to the brink of being totally ruled by a centralized authority. By invoking its authority under the general welfare, commerce, and implied powers clauses in combination with the unlimited taxing authority of the Sixteenth Amendment, the federal government can now impose restrictions on all individual rights.

THE HYBRID SOCIETY IN AMERICA is composed of four classes coexisting side-by-side in two forms of government. It has evolved from the commonly acknowledged three into four economic and social classes. There are the three classes that are usually described by social studies; these are the poor, middle, and wealthy. As a result of the shift to centralized government a fourth can be added, the governing class.

Most descriptions of the first three classes are based upon their economic status. The wealthy have greater social networks and opportunities. Wealthy children have more prospects for training on how to manage and direct their privileges in their different forms. Subsequently, they are able to accumulate even more wealth.

The poor, on the other hand, have the least amount of wealth, and in the United States today they generally receive some form of welfare distribution from the government. When the poor receive welfare assistance in its many forms, their ability to accumulate wealth is limited by government regulations. In order to remain qualified for their assistance, they are not allowed to have more than a trivial amount of assets. A common asset threshold for individuals without disabilities is about $2,000. When faced with the loss of benefits, many of them will not attempt to improve their economic situation, and so they become slaves for life, often for generations entangled in the welfare system.

The middle class is the backbone of America. These individuals are focused on income to meet their daily requirements. Today, many in this classification are able to earn more than is needed for shelter, food, and clothing, and so they accumulate extras such as electronics, a larger home, cars, boats, and other unnecessary objects. Generally, the accumulation of wealth for these folks is in their savings for a rainy day, or retirement. It amounts to a home and a small amount for retirement income.

Now consider the governing class. They principally fit economically into the middle and wealthy classes, but how they obtain their wealth, and how they are affected by the rules of US society are different. These persons have developed pay and benefits systems attached to the standard federal employees program, but enhanced further for their particular self interests. They have used the advantages of representation to develop their private interests while pretending to continue the liberty established by the Constitution. The people of the governing class, which includes all elected representatives, appointed bureaucrats, and the entrenched staff people that work and live in the center city of government, are removed from the daily struggles of American citizens. It appears they have little understanding of the total impact of their tax laws and welfare gifts on the lives of those they are pledged to fairly represent. The writing left behind by the nation's founders indicates they were completely aware of the danger of the evolution of representatives into a governing class. Human behavior was little different from today, and the early leaders cautioned of this problem more than two hundred years ago.

The development of the governing, or ruling, class is tied to the growth of the dependent American culture. These career politicians and federal employees control the dependent class by spending the productive wealth of the working free classes. The governing class has become a large and powerful part of American society, and unless the free, self-governing people of the country take steps to contain the government, then it is likely that a huge, centralized government will be the eventual result, with no truly free society left in existence.

After years of new government programs and class arguments the United States has developed into two societies. There is the welfare society, which is something akin to a socialist existence, and there is the free society that contributes to the welfare society; it is the counter culture that resembles a capitalist system. Those working in the capitalist industrial system for most of their lives tried constantly to be self-sufficient, provide for their families, and grow in the future. In return for honest work they received a paycheck that was reduced by a certain percentage to help sustain the welfare society.

So society today has evolved into two groups, or two systems, and the governing class keeps these systems at odds with one another. The more that is poured into caring for the welfare and entitlement classes, the more these classes demand, and the more the governing class uses the conflict to maintain its own position in society. The net result is a hybrid society. It's a combination of many people living as free as they possibly can under the burden of a demanding tax system while trying to work to their potential (taxpayers), and a second society of citizens that is incapable or unmotivated to care for itself (non-taxpayers). The folks that are not able to provide for themselves, and the subculture of individuals that are able but don't choose to provide their own care, are more willing to give up liberty for security, even if it means stripping freedoms from the working group that provides the security.

The unfortunate consequence of a hybrid society is that both groups are slaves, trapped in servitude to the government. The pseudo-free element is buried in regulations, taxes, and government control of a large part of their private lives. Conversely, the socialized element has given up, surrendering their freedom for a pacifier handed to them by the governing class.

The government of today has been transformed into a monstrous system with tentacles reaching into virtually every facet of daily life. It now provides housing, food, and income for a large part of the citizenry, and many of these folks pay no income tax into the system. Robin Hood representatives frequently speak of taking from the rich and giving to the poor. They want to level the economic situation so that all are about the same, or virtually the same. Obviously, the counter argument is that this abuses personal freedoms. These conflicting arguments have continued for ages.

THE AMERICAN WELFARE STATE hijacks the sacred unalienable right of the individual conscience. When one group, such as the governing class, can force another group, such as working Americans, to provide benefits to a third group, such as the welfare society, then the rights of working Americans to determine whether, how, and whom they should support with their income has been violated. This is the state of affairs that was created by the adoption of federal spending for human resources.

The welfare system of government support has grown steadily

throughout US history, but from 1932 to 1975 it grew at an extraordinary pace. The extensive menu of welfare programs includes supplementary income, food stamps, health care, housing support, education assistance, disability payments, and it's growing. On the surface it's a benevolent plan to help those in need. In reality, it has become a way of life for a certain segment of society. Many recipients have lived on their government benefits for three or more generations. It has simply become the way they live, and many have no desire to change. For those who might want to escape, it is nearly impossible. They can't save, because if they accumulate too much in assets they will forfeit their government benefits. The same thing happens as soon as they find a job. The majority of these citizens languish in their poverty with no chance, or incentive, for escape. It becomes a reverse of the American dream; they are barred from improving their lot in life. Instead of serfs to a feudal lord, they have become serfs to the governing class.

CENTRALIZED DEMOCRACY, sometimes called social democracy, has developed for many years, and some Americans believe the United States is nearing its transition to this form of government. The ideal of this type of government is that government provides security for everything and relief from life's responsibilities. In order to achieve this, the people elect a central governing class and give it authority to control everything from communication, transportation, education, and the economy, to the degree of taxation and how it will be distributed. It is a government by the rule of bureaucratic boards, as opposed to the rule of common law by a self-governing people.

The idea of equality for all is sold to the people, but instead of the people making their own laws in the forum of self-government, an elite group of philosophers, educators and intellectuals, and career politicians decide and enforce the laws. It is the governing class that decides what is equality for all. It awards vested rights to those it decides deserve them. The crucial tradeoff in this form of government is security for freedom. Unalienable freedoms are trampled as the ruling class makes the decisions in proxy for Providence. It is a seductive idea that government will provide a job for everyone, with food, clothing, housing, and medical care throughout their lives. The problem looms that everyone must be treated the same, must act the same, and have the same values as those established by the central government.

Taxes, especially progressive taxes, are the ultimate power of a central government. The central bureau chiefs in power decide the degree of taxation and how the funds will be distributed to the people. Those who fail to comply with the decisions of the central city will be penalized. In an effort to keep everything equal, a centralized government directs all people to the same aims in life, the same thoughts, the same moral codes, and a common purpose. The view of individualism is replaced with the conviction that all people have the same wishes or at least are willing to subvert the wish of the individual for the good of all.

Government by a ruling class is punctuated by economic control and restriction of personal choices. When fully developed, central government controls production and the economy, which is the ultimate control of human life itself. Government agencies or boards become the dominant source of rulemaking. Individual status and income will be established by the central government. In reality only the bureaucrats will be free to grow and achieve. The aim of the ordinary citizen will be reduced to seeking a position of privilege. Ultimately, the elite will decide the control of individual destiny and could be as oppressive as the worst dictator.

In contrast, a pure democracy promises equal liberty for all, versus the social democracy promises of equal restraint for all. A democratic republic is an assembly that is open to every individual, that is, there are no restrictions on who may join or run for election. In a centralized democracy the assemblies are open only to those individuals that agree with the ideals of the majority.

The transition to American central authority is nearing completion. The American founders warned that their formula for freedom through a democratic republic could be lost in a single generation. As soon as the people learn they can vote themselves benefits the government grows and assumes a greater role. These forces combine into the smug idea that the central city knows more about life and what is best for America's citizens. Today, the government regulates food, housing, health care, business, education, and the environment; it's just about everything. All that remains are the Bill of Rights.

THE CONSTITUTION REMAINS STEADFAST. It is still there for freedom-loving citizens. There is still time to reverse the transformation of America, but the possibility of total government control is on the horizon. The stage was set when the constitutionality of the Patient Protection and Affordable Care Act was upheld. The constitutional provisions to lay and collect a progressive income tax were cited as the basis for the decision. When the Sixteenth Amendment to the Constitution was passed, it established the authority to directly tax individuals disproportionately and for different reasons. The Court ruled that this tax system could be employed to force citizens to choose whether to seek health care insurance or pay a tax penalty.

The fearsome danger to American freedom is the collective authority claimed by the federal government using the Sixteenth Amendment and three clauses of the general powers of Congress; these are the general welfare, commerce, and implied powers clauses. It has been ruled that Congress may make any law for the general welfare of all citizens. Similarly, the government may regulate commerce, which has been defined as any flow, or intended flow, of trade or services across state lines; it now encompasses almost any human activity. The implied powers clause has been interpreted to mean that Congress may make any law necessary to enforce the Constitution. The combination of interpretations of these four provisions of the Constitution may leave an opening for Congress to control every aspect of American life. For example, if the Congress should decide to restrict gun ownership, it would likely be possible today by citing these four parts of the Constitution, despite the guarantees of the Second Amendment. This could be accomplished by establishing a huge tax penalty on gun ownership. Citizens could continue to own guns, but there would be a tax penalty to go with it, say something extraordinary such as $10,000 per firearm. These same federal restrictions on general welfare, commerce, implied powers, and progressive taxes could be used on anything the central government may decide it needs to control.

These examples demonstrate the growth of the governing class into a large and powerful part of the hybrid society, and unless the free, self-governing people of the country take steps to contain it, then it is likely that an all-powerful centralized government will be the eventual result, with no free society left in existence.

Americans must make choices and act to reclaim their authority. Regardless of their choices, constitutional change is the only answer. The powers of Congress must be clearly identified. Terms such as, general welfare, regulate commerce, and powers to make laws must be strictly defined and limited. Repeal of the Sixteenth Amendment would be the greatest restoration of American freedom in its history.

Americans may decide that a society that provides social spending for certain citizens should be continued. If so, then it should be put in the Constitution and controlled with constitutional budget limits. It should not be hidden in an abusive tax code and the vague interpretations of the powers of Congress.

Whatever the choices of Americans, it should be in the open and decided by the people, instead of being implemented by bureaus trying to work around the Constitution. New revisions should leave choices open for future generations. Future society may reject the ideas of the hybrid society, and they should have the right to change the Constitution according to the wishes and public opinion of their generation. This was the vision of the country's founders.

The return to the principles of self-government will soothe the people with a new contentment. The people know they can't judge every particle of government business, but they know an educated public can properly support freedom. The people know when they are free to manage their own affairs, in their own way, and through their own skill and effort, that they can prosper and grow.

The alternative is the path called big government, bureaucracy, or centralized democracy. It means an ignorant society that is controlled by an elite few. It means control by a combination of theorists and slippery negotiators that will try to equalize everyone's lives and put all citizens in the same category. Push back by the citizenry occurs, because it's contrary for the freedom of the human spirit to be restrained. So a split occurs, the country quarrels among itself, consideration for others and compromise are lost, and the cycle continues for an unhappy nation.

On Your Watch
Protecting the Republic

EVERY FREE AMERICAN CITIZEN HAS A DUTY to protect the republic that has been inherited from the framers of the Constitution. Americans must meet their civic duty to fulfill the call for jury duty, to vote in elections, to work and pay taxes, and to keep a vigilant watch of their representatives. It starts with jury duty when called to serve, because the common law jury is the basis of the Constitution and of self-government. It was the vision of the founders to protect the individual from government persecution by establishing the common law jury system. The founders intended that the people make the laws, not the government, and so the American jury system is somewhat of a peculiarity among world governments. Almost no other countries use it. Americans must protect it.

Every American recognizes the privilege to vote for the individuals and propositions of their choice. Few countries offer the opportunities of true self-government, but it has been sustained in the United States for two centuries. Some centralized democracies offer the right to vote, but with restrictions; such as, they may be required to be a member of a certain party before the right to vote is assured. Americans should vote often.

Not every American pays taxes, but every American should strive to pay taxes. Those who live in the country and draw unearned benefits without contributing to the treasury are anchors on the ability of the country to grow and prosper. All Americans should work within their abilities and contribute to the national economy. The individual income tax may be the worst idea in American history, but as long as it exists, every individual must support it. Able-bodied Americans should pay taxes.

After exercising their voting privilege, American citizens must keep tabs on the job their elected officials do in following the Constitution. No individual can be trusted without some sort of checks and balance, whether it is accounting for business activities or making new laws. Many responsible citizens work, pay taxes, vote, and serve on juries, but then fail to remain vigilant of government decisions. Americans must watch.

There is no hope for self-government if the citizens do not participate. Government will endlessly grow larger and assume more authority without the safeguard of vigilant and insistent citizens. Admittedly, the government today has become so large that it is difficult for busy families to follow the antics of the central government, but they must make the effort to watch decisions and keep them within constitutional boundaries.

It is easy to be disillusioned, but it is not a new state of affairs. Comments by Americans from the eighteenth to twentieth century speak of the problem. It has been said that people don't give a damn what the average Senator or Congressman has to say, because most of it is garbage, ignorance, and maneuvering for more power. A member of the White House Cabinet once commented that many in Congress were wholly unfit to serve; some purchased their positions with their wealth, some were of narrow intellect, and some simply used partisan prejudice to advance their careers. Nevertheless, there are honest and courageous public servants, too. In his Pulitzer Prize book, *Profiles In Courage*, Senator John Kennedy tells the stories of eight senators who sacrificed their careers for what they believed to be the common good of the country. One of these inspiring stories concerns Robert A Taft, the Senator from Ohio at the end of World War Two. Senator Taft criticized the Nuremberg Trials of Nazi War Criminals. He believed they were based on ex post facto laws that are prohibited by the US Constitution. Despite the atrocities committed by the Nazi monsters, Senator Taft pointed out that they were being tried against laws that were made "after the fact." It probably cost him the 1948 Republican nomination for president.

The Constitution is the thread that holds the country together and gives each citizen the security of freedom. Each free American must tenaciously protect it.

THE CORE QUESTION is whether individual Americans can make a difference by remaining vigilant of the actions of their elected leaders?

THE HISTORY OF WARNINGS to Americans about the dangers of not participating in self-government began with the forefathers. Three notable personalities were George Washington, the leader of the Revolutionary War and the country's first president, Thomas

Jefferson, the lead author of the Declaration of Independence and the country's third president, and James Madison, recognized as the father of the Constitution and the fourth president of the US. These men brought great experience and wisdom to the ideas of individual freedom and self-government.

George Washington worried about the temptation to work around the Constitution and told his countrymen that the underlying principles of the Constitution must be scrupulously guarded, protected, and preserved. Jefferson agreed and warned future generations that if a nation expects to be ignorant and free, it expects what never will be, and he further cautioned that even in the best forms of government, those entrusted with power would slowly pervert it. James Madison, who melded the ideas of public opinion and self-government, believed that once the people cast their votes, they couldn't rest easy or place unlimited confidence in their representatives.

Ultimately, the forefathers left the chilling warning that without the steady vigilance of responsible citizens, the republic could be lost in one generation.

In modern times the government has become more complicated than the earliest days of operation. Though more difficult to follow, it is even more important that citizens try to keep the government honest, because the more complicated the form of government, the more individual freedom is restricted. The government today is filled with bureaucratic specialists with personal agendas. It is but a short step from specialist to unreasonable authoritarian.

Today, Congress has surrendered much of the power as set forth in the Constitution. There were both efficiency reasons and selfish reasons for the transition, but it means a shift from the power of the people in the Congress, to the power of centralized bureaus and unelected staff members. A single example that receives a lot of attention today is the national budget ceiling. The idea of the debt ceiling was created in 1917. Before that, the Congress approved specific loans individually. It was changed to an aggregate loan amount to eliminate the requirement to review each loan request. Now, the Congress struggles to control the debt ceiling, and the politics between parties and branches of government have caused numerous unpleasant situations for the country.

The debt ceiling is one example of Congress surrendering too much power to other branches of government and allowing departmental rule making to get out of hand. The White House, its Cabinet Departments, and its Administrative staff make laws and penalties for every facet of daily American life.

PROTECTING THE REPUBLIC by a watchful citizen is demonstrated by the inspiring story of Horatio Bunce. Mr. Bunce was presumably a voter in the district represented by Davy Crockett in the early 1800s. He was a farmer, but also a student of the Constitution. He thoroughly watched the activities of his government, and ultimately taught the Congressman a lesson in following the provisions of the Constitution.

The story is an excerpt from *The Life of Colonel David Crockett*, a book by Edward S Ellis. Mr. Ellis was born in 1840, after Davy Crockett fell at the Alamo. He became a teacher and successful author of magazine articles and dime novels that were widely read in his era and for some time afterward. The story of Horatio Bunce was first published in 1867 in *Harper's* magazine before it later became part of the book.

The accuracy of the story is questionable, and it could be historical fiction. The story itself concerns a Congressional bill to provide federal relief to a widow of a naval officer who lost her home in a Georgetown fire. Historical research has shown flaws in the story, including no evidence of a fire in Georgetown in a naval widow's home. There are some records of a fire in Alexandria, but this was before Crockett served in Congress. Also, there is no record of a naval widow, but Crockett is on record opposing a similar appropriation for the family of a General Brown in April 1828. No records of the life of Horatio Bunce have been found, yet.

This story has been widely circulated in print and on the Internet in the last twenty years or so, and it is a great lesson in citizenship. Whether it's true or not, or whether an individual agrees with Bunce's views on charity or not, the important point of the story is the example of an involved citizen. Whether the story is fact or fiction, the example of citizen Bunce stands on its own merit.

Here it is.

NOT YOURS TO GIVE

Taken from:
The Life of Colonel David Crockett,
compiled by Edward S Ellis
(Porter & Coates, 1884)

One day in the House of Representatives, a bill was taken up appropriating money for the benefit of a widow of a distinguished naval officer. Several beautiful speeches had been made in its support. The Speaker was just about to put the question when Crockett arose:

"Mr. Speaker – I have as much respect for the memory of the deceased, and as much sympathy for the sufferings of the living, if suffering there be, as any man in this House, but we must not permit our respect for the dead or our sympathy for a part of the living to lead us into an act of injustice to the balance of the living. I will not go into an argument to prove that Congress has no power to appropriate this money as an act of charity. Every member upon this floor knows it. We have the right, as individuals, to give away as much of our own money as we please in charity; but as members of Congress we have no right so to appropriate a dollar of the public money. Some eloquent appeals have been made to us upon the ground that it is a debt due the deceased. Mr. Speaker, the deceased lived long after the close of the war; he was in office to the day of his death, and I have never heard that the government was in arrears to him.

"Every man in this House knows it is not a debt. We cannot, without the grossest corruption, appropriate this money as the payment of a debt. We have not the semblance of authority to appropriate it as a charity. Mr. Speaker, I have said we have the right to give as much money of our own as we please. I am the poorest man on this floor. I cannot vote for this bill, but I will give one week's pay to the object, and if every member of Congress will do the same, it will amount to more than the bill asks."

He took his seat. Nobody replied. The bill was put upon its passage, and, instead of passing unanimously, as was generally supposed, and as, no doubt, it would, but for that speech, it received but few votes, and, of course, was lost.

Later, when asked by a friend why he had opposed the appropriation, Crockett gave this explanation:

"Several years ago I was one evening standing on the steps of the Capitol with some other members of Congress, when our attention was attracted by a great light over in Georgetown. It was evidently a large fire. We jumped into a hack and drove over as fast as we could. In spite of all that could be done, many houses were burned and many families made houseless, and, besides, some of them had lost all but the clothes they had on. The weather was very cold, and when I saw so many women and children suffering, I felt that something ought to be done for them. The next morning a bill was introduced appropriating $20,000 for their relief. We put aside all other business and rushed it through as soon as it could be done.

"The next summer, when it began to be time to think about the election, I concluded I would take a scout around among the boys of my district. I had no opposition there, but, as the election was some time off, I did not know what might turn up. When riding one day in a part of my district in which I was more of a stranger than any other, I saw a man in a field plowing and coming toward the road. I gauged my gait so that we should meet as he came to the fence. As he came up, I spoke to the man. He replied politely, but, as I thought, rather coldly.

"I began: 'Well, friend, I am one of those unfortunate beings called candidates, and - '

" 'Yes, I know you; you are Colonel Crockett. I have seen you once before, and voted for you the last time you were elected. I suppose you are out electioneering now, but you had better not waste your time or mine. I shall not vote for you again.'

"This was a sockdolager. . . I begged him to tell me what was the matter.

" 'Well, Colonel, it is hardly worth-while to waste time or words upon it. I do not see how it can be mended, but you gave a vote last winter which shows that either you have not capacity to understand the Constitution, or that you are wanting in honesty and firmness to be guided by it. In either case you are not the man to represent me. But I beg your pardon for expressing it in that way. I did not intend to avail myself of the privilege of the constituent to speak plainly to a candidate for the purpose of insulting or wounding you. I intend by it only to say that your understanding of the Constitution is very different from mine; and I will say to you what, but for my rudeness, I should not have said, that I believe you to be honest. . . But an understanding of the Constitution different from mine I cannot overlook, because the Constitution, to be worth anything, must be held sacred, and rigidly observed in all its provisions. The man who wields power and misinterprets it is the more dangerous the more honest he is.'

" 'I admit the truth of all you say, but there must be some mistake about it, for I do not remember that I gave any vote last winter upon any constitutional question.'

" 'No, Colonel, there's no mistake. Though I live here in the backwoods and seldom go from home, I take the papers from Washington and read very carefully all the proceedings of Congress. My papers say that last winter you voted for a bill to appropriate $20,000 to some sufferers by a fire in Georgetown. Is that true?'

" 'Well, my friend; I may as well own up. You have got me there. But certainly nobody will complain that a great and rich country like ours should give the insignificant sum of $20,000 to relieve its suffering women and children, particularly with a full and overflowing Treasury, and I am sure, if you had been there, you would have done just as I did.'

" 'It is not the amount, Colonel, that I complain of; it is the principle. In the first place, the government ought to have in the Treasury no more than enough for its legitimate purposes. But that has nothing to do with the question. The power of collecting and disbursing money at pleasure is the most dangerous power that can be intrusted to man, particularly under our system of collecting revenue by a tariff, which reaches every man in the country, no matter how poor he may be, and the poorer he is the more he pays in proportion to his means. What is worse, it presses upon him without his knowledge where the weight centers, for there is not a man in the United States who can ever guess how much he pays to the government. So you see, that while you are contributing to relieve one, you are drawing it from thousands who are even worse off than he. If you had the right to give anything, the amount was simply a matter of discretion with you, and you had as much right to give $20,000,000 as $20,000. If you have the right to give to one, you have the right to give to all; and, as the Constitution neither defines charity nor stipulates the amount, you are at liberty to give to any and everything which you may believe, or profess to believe, is a charity, and to any amount you may think proper. You will very easily perceive what a wide door this would open for fraud and corruption and favoritism, on the one hand, and for robbing the people on the other. No, Colonel, Congress has no right to give charity. Individual members may give as much of their own money as they please, but they have no right to touch a dollar of the public money for that purpose. If twice as many houses had been burned in this country as in Georgetown, neither you nor any other member of Congress would have thought of appropriating a dollar for our relief. There are about two hundred and forty members of Congress. If they had shown their sympathy for the sufferers by contributing each one week's pay, it would have made over $13,000. There are plenty of wealthy men in and around Washington who could have given $20,000 without depriving themselves of even a luxury of life. The congressmen chose to keep their own money, which, if reports be true, some of them spend not very creditably; and the people about Washington, no doubt, applauded you for relieving them from the necessity of giving by giving what was not yours to give. The people have delegated Congress, by the Constitution, the power to do certain things. To do these, it is authorized to collect and pay moneys, and for nothing else. Everything beyond this is usurpation, and a violation of the Constitution.

" 'So you see, Colonel, you have violated the Constitution in what I consider a vital point. It is a precedent fraught with danger to the country, for when Congress once begins to stretch its power beyond the limits of the Constitution, there is not limit to it, and no security for the people. I have no doubt you acted honestly, but that does not make it any better, except as far as you are personally concerned, and you see that I cannot vote for you.'

"I tell you I felt streaked. I saw if I should have opposition, and this man should go to talking, he would set others to talking, and in that district I was a gone fawn-skin. I could not answer him, and the fact is, I was so fully convinced that he was right, I did not want to. But I must satisfy him, and I said to him:

" 'Well, my friend, you hit the nail upon the head when you said I had not sense enough to understand the Constitution. I intended to be guided by it, and thought I had studied it fully. I have heard many speeches in Congress about the powers of Congress, but what you have said here at your plow has got more hard, sound sense in it than all the fine speeches I ever heard. If I had ever taken the view of it that you have, I would have put my head into the fire before I would have given that vote; and if I ever vote for another unconstitutional law I wish I may be shot.'

"He laughingly replied: 'Yes, Colonel, you have sworn to that once before, but I will trust you again upon one condition. You say that you are convinced that your vote was wrong. Your acknowledgment of it will do more good than beating you for it. If, as you go around the district, you will tell people about this vote, and that you are satisfied it was wrong, I will not only vote for you, but will do what I can to keep down opposition, and, perhaps, I may exert some little influence in that way.'

" 'If I don't,' said I, 'I wish I may be shot; and to convince you that I am in earnest in what I say I will come back this way in a week or ten days, and if you will get up a gathering of the people, I will make a speech to them. Get up a barbecue, and I will pay for it.'

" 'No, Colonel, we are not rich people in this section, but we have plenty of provisions to contribute for a barbecue, and some to spare for those who have none. The push of crops will be over in a few days, and we can then afford a day for a barbecue. This is Thursday; I will see to getting it up on Saturday week. Come to my house on Friday, and we will go together, and I promise you a very respectable crowd to see and hear you.'

" 'Well, I will be here. But one thing more before I say good-by. I must know your name.'

" 'My name is Bunce.'

" 'Not Horatio Bunce?'

" 'Yes.'

" 'Well, Mr. Bunce, I never saw you before, though you say you have seen me, but I know you very well. I am glad I have met you, and very proud that I may hope to have you for my friend.'

"It was one of the luckiest hits of my life that I met him. He mingled but little with the public, but was widely known for his remarkable intelligence and incorruptible integrity, and for a heart brimful and running over with kindness and benevolence, which showed themselves not only in words but in acts. He was the oracle of the whole country around him, and his fame had extended far beyond the circle of his immediate acquaintance. Though I had never met him before, I had heard much of him, and but for this meeting it is very likely I should have had opposition, and had been beaten. One thing is very certain, no man could now stand up in that district under such a vote.

"At the appointed time I was at his house, having told our conversation to every crowd I had met, and to every man I stayed all night with, and I found that it gave the people an interest and a confidence in me stronger than I had ever seen manifested before.

"Though I was considerably fatigued when I reached his house, and, under ordinary circumstances, should have gone early to bed, I kept him up until midnight, talking about the principles and affairs of government, and got more real, true knowledge of them than I had got all my life before.

"I have known and seen much of him since, for I respect him – no, that is not the word – I reverence and love him more than any living man, and I go to see him two or three times every year; and I will tell you, sir, if every one who professes to be a Christian lived and acted and enjoyed it as he does, the religion of Christ would take the world by storm.

"But to return to my story. The next morning we went to the barbecue, and, to my surprise, found about a thousand men there. I met a good many whom I had not known before, and they and my friend introduced me around until I had got pretty well acquainted – at least, they all knew me.

"In due time notice was given that I would speak to them. They gathered up around a stand that had been erected. I opened my speech by saying:

" 'Fellow-citizens – I present myself before you today feeling like a new man. My eyes have lately been opened to truths which ignorance or prejudice, or both, had heretofore hidden from my view. I feel that I can today offer you the ability to render you more valuable service than I have ever been able to render before. I am here today more for the purpose of acknowledging my error than to seek your votes. That I should make this acknowledgement is due to myself as well as to you. Whether you will vote for me is a matter for your consideration only.'

"I went on to tell them about the fire and my vote for the appropriation and then told them why I was satisfied it was wrong. I closed by saying:

" 'And now, fellow-citizens, it remains only for me to tell you that the most of the speech you have listened to with so much interest was simply a repetition of the arguments by which your neighbor, Mr. Bunce, convinced me of my error.

" 'It is the best speech I ever made in my life, but he is entitled to the credit for it. And now I hope he is satisfied with his convert and that he will get up here and tell you so.'

"He came upon the stand and said:

" 'Fellow-citizens – it affords me great pleasure to comply with the request of Colonel Crockett. I have always considered him a thoroughly honest man, and I am satisfied that he will faithfully perform all that he has promised you today.'

"He went down, and there went up from that crowd such a shout for Davy Crockett as his name never called forth before.

"I am not much given to tears, but I was taken with a choking then and felt some big drops rolling down my cheeks. And I tell you now that the remembrance of those few words spoken by such a man, and the honest, hearty shout they produced, is worth more to me than all the honors I have received and all the reputation I have ever made, or ever shall make, as a member of Congress.

"Now, sir," concluded Crockett, "you know why I made that speech yesterday.

"There is one thing now to which I will call your attention. You remember that I proposed to give a week's pay. There are in that House many very wealthy men – men who think nothing of spending a week's pay, or a dozen of them, for a dinner or a wine party when they have something to accomplish by it. Some of those same men made beautiful speeches upon the great debt of gratitude which the country owed the deceased – a debt which could not be paid by money – and the insignificance and worthlessness of money, particularly so insignificant a sum as $10,000, when weighed against the honor of the nation. Yet not one of them responded to my proposition. Money with them is nothing but trash when it is to come out of the people. But it is the one great thing for which most of them are striving, and many of them sacrifice honor, integrity, and justice to obtain it."

Here the story ends. Horatio Bunce didn't let his civic responsibility end after he cast his vote. He monitored the activity of the government, and when he believed it strayed from the provisions of the Constitution, he resolved to remove the offenders with his vote. Citizen Bunce recognized the awesome power given to Congress by the people to collect and disburse money. Notice that this story occurred before the progressive income tax, so Mr. Bunce reminded Congressman Crockett that collecting revenue by tariff affected all citizens. This meant that giving charity to one meant taking from another that might be worse off. The evidence of this situation is apparent today at the tax desk when one citizen is seen struggling to juggle bills while meeting a tax obligation, but another pays no tax, receives an extra tax credit boost, and lives at a better standard than the low-income tax payer. Horatio Bunce knew there was no provision in the Constitution that gave Congress the right to give charity, and he recognized that charity opens the door for fraud, corruption, and favoritism. The story is an excellent lesson in civic responsibility for citizens and representatives alike.

THE CONCLUSION for all Americans is to know the Constitution, vote often, and then follow the actions of all branches of government. Start with the local Congressman and Senators, and then examine the actions of the President, the Cabinet, their staffs and policies. Whether or not the story of Horatio Bunce is fiction, it is an example to be taken to heart by all citizens.

Know the Constitution and form a personal understanding. The subject of disaster relief is a good starting point. These days, it's political suicide to be opposed to government spending for disaster relief. But is it truly constitutional, despite the conclusions of a handful of elite theorists? The decision should be by the people.

Be a responsible citizen, follow the calling to jury duty, to vote, to work and pay taxes, and to keep a vigilance at all levels of government. Horatio Bunce is a remarkable example of responsible citizenship. If this type of citizenship became dominant in America, there likely would be many new faces in public office, and a different view of the Constitution. Citizens are the government. Federal officers are merely their representatives.

Progressive Income Tax
A Case for Repeal

MOST AMERICANS BORN AFTER 1930 may think the progressive income tax system utilized in the United States today has been the tax system used since the beginning of federal operations in 1789. Others may have learned otherwise in school but have forgotten. Almost all younger taxpayers believe taxes are necessary and that the current method of taxing all individual income is the only way to do it. Of course taxes are necessary to support federal operations, but the direct progressive income tax system has not always been the system used. In fact, it's new, admittedly about 100 years new, but for most of the preceding half of the country's history, the progressive income tax system was unconstitutional.

The idea of a progressive tax on income was repugnant to the framers of the Constitution, because they believed it would be impossible to fairly assess and collect from citizens. The citizens of the country in 1913 saw it differently, however, and ratified the Sixteenth Amendment to the Constitution to permit the application of the direct progressive method of taxing individual citizens. This modification of the Constitution may have changed American culture more than any other system in its history, and it has become the single biggest breach of true American freedom.

Its sinister restriction of freedom occurs in at least three ways: it enlarges the centralized government; it chains individual citizens to the federal government; and, it is disproportionately unfair. The growth of the federal government correlates to some extent to the start of the progressive income tax. It has enabled a governing class of bureaucrats to assume a role of deciding how private individuals should spend their money and live their lives, and it empowers and enlarges the centralized government. A common question among Americans today is, "Why is the country so polarized and divided?" The brilliant Scottish philosopher from the eighteenth century, David Hume, suggested that the root cause of political factions is centralized government. The situation in America today makes a good case for his observation as the citizens are deprived of their rights to decide for themselves at the local level, by an ever-expanding central government that seeks a common answer for all segments of society. The income tax splits the country and pits citizens against one another.

The American citizen today is tied for life to the federal government through the requirement to report in each year. Common citizens are expected to become accountants, to learn abstract accounting terms and rules, and keep copious records of their activity. The result for too many is that they are tied for years with debt to the government, and for a large majority, it is because they simply couldn't understand the rules. This awful tax system leaves Americans disheartened and resentful. It drains the joy out of American life, leaving a nation that can never be truly content with this specter lurking over them.

For the few that are able to negotiate the system, or the more who pay a tax preparer to negotiate it for them, there is the unfailing disbelief at the inequality that abounds in its rules. There are breaks for some, but none for others. Taxpayers are unable to understand why some get favors, but others don't. As long as federal lawmakers sit in isolated offices, in an isolated central city, and continue to develop disproportionate taxes, they can never be fair, and will remain an unfair characteristic.

With 100 years of experience using this monstrosity, perhaps now is the time for Americans to review whether the use of the progressive income tax system should be continued.

THE CORE QUESTION, then, is should the purpose of a tax system be to manipulate the behavior of citizens and punish those who don't fall in line with the preferences of government, or should the tax system be used strictly to raise revenue to operate the federal government?

TAX HISTORY begins with the founding fathers in their search for a fair and equitable way to obtain money to run the federal government. Of course, they believed the sole purpose of taxes was to raise revenue. Naturally, the idea of using taxes to control behavior and take personal fortunes was not seriously considered when the Constitution was framed. In the eyes of the founders, the whole purpose of government was to provide for three services: defense; fair trade and commerce; and, a court system of fair and equitable laws. Nothing more was expected, and only enough tax revenue to adequately support these activities was intended.

Two types of taxation were considered when developing the Constitution. There could be a direct tax placed directly on a person, property, or their income; or, they could use indirect taxes on finished goods or work-in-progress that is passed on to consumers. The founders eventually wrote both methods into the Constitution, but with an important restriction on direct taxes. They believed it was impossible to fairly assess and collect a varying direct tax, so the Fourth Clause of the Ninth Section of the First Article was included that reads, "No capitation, or other direct tax, shall be laid, unless in proportion to the census or enumeration herein directed to be taken." It meant that if a direct tax were to be used, all citizens must pay the same rate.

As a result, the federal government largely operated using duties and excise taxes for the first half of its existence. In fact, it leaned heavily on liquor sales, and in 1791 the Whiskey Rebellion in Western Pennsylvania posed a problem for the new nation in a dispute over using liquor taxes to pay down the huge debt accumulated during the Revolutionary War.

After about fifty years of American government, new communist ideas became popular in parts of the world. In 1848 Karl Marx and Friedrich Engels published the *Communist Manifesto*, which was their platform of the Communist League. The communist movement favored progressive taxes, and step two of their "Ten Steps to Change to Communism," states "Impose a heavy progressive or graduated tax." It was their view that the only way to implement a fair society would be to break down the existing one in ten steps, and one of the more important ways suggested was to redistribute property and income using the progressive income tax. Though not immediately accepted in America, the seed was planted in the minds of the American progressive mindset.

America survived about seventy years before the first direct taxes were assessed. In 1861 a direct tax of three percent of all income over $800 was established to offset the tremendous Civil War debt. Wars are the chief cause of debt for the American government, and the Civil War was not an exception. Following this, in 1894, the government tried direct taxes in an effort to make up revenue lost through tariff reductions, which was the prime source of federal revenue at that time. They settled on two percent on income over $4,000, but less than ten percent of US households made that kind of money, so it slid through without much resistance. About a year later, though, the government tried to include taxes on real estate rent, interest income, and other specific types of income, but it didn't survive. The Supreme Court struck it down as unconstitutional, because it was not a uniform direct tax. As a result, Congress decided equal distribution of direct taxes was impractical, and so it ended. The country was saved by the foresight of the Constitution.

About this same time, around 1890, the prohibition movement was really picking up steam during the progressive era of purity. Their progress was stymied, however, because the government relied heavily on liquor taxes for operational revenue. The prohibitionists realized that a personal tax was needed to replace the liquor excise tax and open the door for prohibition legislation. Ultimately, the nation ratified the Sixteenth Amendment to the Constitution in 1913, and the new income tax replaced alcohol taxes as an important source to fund the federal government. The prohibitionists had won, and in 1919 the Eighteenth Amendment was ratified to outlaw liquor, which was implemented in 1920. US citizens realized it was a mistake, though; after only thirteen years the Twenty-first Amendment reversed the Eighteenth Amendment in 1933. Unfortunately, the larger damage caused by the progressive tax amendment remained on the books.

The progressive tax system has grown insidiously since its inception. Tax rates have exploded, instructions to tax payers are a thousand times larger, and withholding was added to it. The top tax rate in 1913 was seven percent above $500,000, and some legislators wanted a cap in the Amendment, but they were assured it would never be necessary. Wars raised it again: in World War One, the top rate was 77%, in World War Two it reached 94%, and in the 1960s and 1970s the top rate hovered around 77% again. The number of instructions for a tax return increased from four in 1913 to 4,000 today. The ultimate insult, though, came during World War Two when the pay-as-you-go system developed into the withholding system still in use today. This robbery deprives citizens of their earnings before they are paid.

The history of the progressive tax system continues today with a bloated and convoluted system that confounds accountants, politicians, and taxpayers alike. The administrative costs are enormous, and the cost to operate the IRS swallows about eighteen percent of the annual tax revenues collected. A program with administrative costs this high would be urgently reviewed in the business world.

CENTRALIZED GOVERNMENT is the first restriction of freedom resulting from progressive tax methods. A governing class was born and empowered by the inherent provisions for controlling tax rates and gifts, such as credits and deductions. The populous learned quickly that it could vote itself tax benefits, so the governing class became entrenched by using this provision. The governing class became an example of the feudal systems of old where the Lord of the Manor cared for his subjects, except the governing class used the progressive tax system to take care of its subjects with other people's money. It has become a self-fulfilling system that herds Americans like sheep into dependence on the federal government. A second element of the governing class is the lobbying business that utilizes the tax system and depends on it for maintaining its strangle hold, until today the lobbying business has become a revolving door for congressional legislators leaving office to rake in yet more riches at the expense of the public. Ending the progressive tax system could remove one element of abuse by lobbyist groups. If the money goes, they will, too.

The net result of control by a governing class is that it uses the progressive tax system for control of the people, not for raising revenue. Sure, it needs the revenue, but it has a lock on that today. Today their role as Lords of the Manor has expanded the idea of vested rights. In its zeal to maintain its position, the governing class has blurred the distinction between vested and unalienable rights until a lot of Americans can't tell the difference either. Of course, the unalienable rights are the God-given birthrights guaranteed by the Constitution, but vested, or statutory, rights are conferred by governments, and can be reclaimed. Now, the progressive income tax system has become a perverted method of bestowing vested rights, such as welfare, housing, education assistance, and health care. In addition to doling out vested gifts, the governing class uses the tax system to guide, nudge, and direct taxpayers to follow their rules. Mortgage a house, save for education, buy an electric car, or make specified home improvements; these are the subtle ways the governing class decides what is best for its subjects. Further, Americans are encouraged to depend on the government by seeking free benefits, such as the earned income credits and other give-away programs.

The advent of the progressive income tax system has changed the role of the tax system from collecting necessary operating revenue to manipulation and control by a governing class that is growing in numbers and power.

CITIZENS ARE CHAINED to the government by the progressive tax system. The income tax system presupposes all citizens operate on a money economy. It requires that they understand receipts, expenses, and profit, and it demands that they keep reliable records. There is no escape. Anyone with reportable income is bound to the central city by these chains and must report to it.

The loss of personal income during a lifetime is staggering. Money paid by individuals inhibits their ability to save and avoid debt. With the practice of withholding the money from their wages before they receive it, they have lost the control of a segment of their labor to the federalists. Worse, many trust in their employers and this system to cover their tax bill, only to find themselves bound with the heavier chains of debt when it fails.

The country's founders, in their vision of freedom, would be astounded by the annual ritual of each citizen reporting in to the federal giant, and its effect on the lives of each person. Taxpayers nervously face the annual tax return. They are subjected to a terrible burden, and to not too insignificant terror for some. They struggle to be on time and worry, "Will I owe this year? How will I pay?" This is not how a free people should live.

For those who owe, it is often the result of debt traps that are built into the twists of exceptions to the rules. Often windfall income is the culprit. Folks who cash an annuity or retirement plan may owe extraordinary tax payments, descendants of farmers who sell the family farm or other property could owe a substantial amount, and lottery or gambling winners may find themselves in tax brackets they never imagined. If the money hasn't been set aside, then there are major problems for the lucky, but hapless person.

Other innocent and surprising debt traps include drawing

unemployment, cancellation of debt, self-employment, or simply having a child leave the nest. Unbelievably, folks out of work can find themselves short at tax time. They simply draw unemployment when out of work, but later find that they owe a good portion of it to the federal coffers. The IRS considers cancellation of debt by a credit card company as income, and most folks are surprised to learn this little nuance that frequently results with money owed. For the ambitious Americans who choose to strike out in their own business, there is a big surprise for those who are unprepared. In the first year, many learn the importance of quarterly payments and planning ahead, and often the plan includes monthly payments to the US Treasury for the debt owed from their first year. A last example of people frequently caught in tax debt occurs when a child reaches the age of seventeen and leaves home. The taxpayer's child tax credit is terminated, and their deduction as a dependent may be lost, but the vast majority doesn't adjust their withholding, especially in the low income demographic, and find themselves wallowing in a large debt to pay off over three to five years, or longer.

Perhaps one of the more cruel effects of the tax system falls on senior citizens. These folks are overwhelmed by the transition rules of Individual Retirement Arrangement (IRA) and 401(k) accounts. It's boggling to a sharp and youthful mind, let alone an aged individual attempting to decipher the rules of required minimum distributions, and so forth.

It is never enough, however. Even with all the twists and turns in this labyrinth the Congress has created, it continues to add more. Now with the mandatory requirements for maintaining health insurance, taxpayers will have yet another confusion to deal with, one more debt trap to avoid, and one more requirement to report in to the IRS with an informational return to prove they are in compliance with the laws of the governing class.

TAXES ARE UNFAIR AND UNEQUAL for taxpayers serving the progressive income tax system. The supporters of redistributive taxes claim each American should pay their fair share. What, though, is a fair share? Should citizens be required to pay a disproportionate share of their income, just because they don't have enough deductions or credits to avoid paying more? The founders believed all Americans have a natural duty of contributing an equal share for the necessities of society. Those who believe in unequal payments are those who also believe in soaking the rich. But who are the rich? A lot of taxpayers join the "rich for a year" club when they receive windfall income from cashing in their own savings in an annuity, or any number of other circumstances that can quickly vault a household into the top income bracket.

Worse, though, a lot of Americans pay no income taxes. Is this a fair share when they contribute nothing to the operation of the country? Isn't this like living with parents rent-free? Often these are the low-income households that receive free gifts, such as earned income credit, or child tax credit, but also included are households with income in the top one percent that pay no income tax because of offsetting deductions and other situations. Over forty percent of American households do not pay income tax today. Is this a fair share?

Inequities abound with itemized deductions. An alternative concept of itemized deductions is that for every deduction taken, another taxpayer who receives no deduction makes up the difference. This is particularly true in cases of mortgage deductions, meal per-diem deductions, and travel mileage deductions. A family that saves and pays for a home receives no mortgage deduction, but a family that doesn't save, but borrows most of the cost, receives tremendous deductions. Their neighbors help them pay for their mortgages. Which is paying a fair share?

Other rewards are available for health care deductions. The IRS maintains a list of covered illnesses and procedures, just like an insurance company. A taxpayer can deduct an abortion under the provisions for prenatal care, for birth control measures, and fertility enhancement procedures. Who pays for this? It comes from those who have no offsetting deductions. Who pays a fair share?

The reward and punitive rules further cloud the fair share question. For example, some taxpayers receive up to half of their retirement savings contributions returned in the form of a credit, while others receive nothing and pay the credit for those receiving the benefit. Taxpayers who adopt children can receive enormous rewards, while on the punitive side, taxpayers who use tanning beds pay more as a result of the special taxes on their choice to tan. Who pays a fair share?

The progressive tax system and its fair share argument is the chief cause of class jealousy in the United States. The important point is that taxpayers without deductions pay for the deductions and credits of their fellow taxpayers. It doesn't come from the government. When national revenue is reduced by credits and deductions, then it must be compensated by a tax rate adjustment for those without benefits. Is this fair share?

The ultimate unfairness and restriction of personal freedom occurs each year when taxpayers must pay tax preparers, bookkeepers, and accountants to help them satisfy the demands of the system. Americans are stripped of the control of the money they earn. No American should be forced to pay for help. Any system that causes this situation takes the joy out of American citizenship.

THE ONLY CONCLUSION for restoring fairness to the duty of contributing to the national treasury is to scrap the current system. The American right to happiness cannot flourish under this oppressive tax system. Taxpayers today serve the system; the tax system doesn't serve the citizens. The purest solution is to abolish the grip of this repulsive law. By ratifying a Twenty-eighth Amendment to repeal the mistake of the Sixteenth, the error will be corrected in a manner similar to the correction of the prohibition law. The difference is it took only thirteen years to correct the drinking law, but 100 years have passed since the tax law was approved. It is firmly entrenched and will be difficult to reverse.

Abolishing the Sixteenth Amendment will return the federal government to operating on duties, tariffs, and excise tax. Its basis generally would be the production of the country. Each improvement in the value of a commodity or service would result in a federal tax. A simple example would occur when a timber business cuts a tree and sells it, there would be a federal tax. When the lumbering operation converts it and sells lumber to a builder, there would be a federal tax. Continuing with the builder then, when the lumber is used to construct a house that is sold, there would be a tax on the sale of the house. Businesses would still be required to maintain records and accounting. Freed individuals would pay their fair share through their purchases.

Seven states in the US have successfully operated without imposing the burden of income taxes on their citizens, and two more do not tax ordinary income, but do tax intangible income, such as interest. Of course, these states turn to other revenue sources to pay operating expenses. They utilize sales taxes, fuel taxes, property taxes, and other tax methods, while their residents are free of record keeping requirements and reporting in to the government. Alaska, Florida, Nevada, South Dakota, Texas, Washington, and Wyoming have shown how possible and practical this can be.

The IRS will still be needed, but there will be a mammoth savings with the reduction in size that can be made. Their job will be reduced to monitoring business reports and policing lawbreakers. No more direct contact with individual citizens, and the workload of following millions of individual returns will be up in smoke.

It is time to abandon the tax revisionist theories. Senior citizens have witnessed abundant tax revisions in their lifetimes. Each time, the tax rates and abuses creep back, and usually are worse than before. The reason lies with the Congress. It is common for legislators to turn to tax solutions when a problem is presented in session. Farmers need help, give them tax relief. Entertainers need relief, give them tax deductions. Students need living expenses, give them tax credits. When the progressive tax system is repealed, Congress will have to turn to new, and hopefully less damaging solutions.

The flat tax has been suggested as an alternative. Presumably this would be a progressive hybrid, because there would remain differing brackets. But even if it were settled on one bracket, Americans would remain encumbered by record keeping, rules, and reporting in. Further, special deductions and favors won't be eliminated, and slowly but surely, it would join the other revision methods to become a complicated dragon again, like many preceding attempts to simplify the system. None of the provisions of the flat tax, of course, would result in a reduction of the size of the IRS; it would remain as ever.

The alternative argument to the flat tax has been the fair tax. This idea corresponds somewhat to the indirect tax method used by the country for its first one hundred years. It would amount to a national sales tax on purchases. Citizens would not have to check in with the revenue service, and they would take home the entire amount of their pay. It could be a good first step, but it leaves the states with the power to continue requiring state income tax returns, and it leaves the door cracked for a federal return to the progressive system. Only a constitutional amendment can totally reverse this beast.

Of course, it is a vacant hope that Congress would initiate a constitutional amendment to repeal the tax law. But a slim chance is possible through a tranquil revolution of the people. Not guns, riots, or demonstrations. An independent Constitutional Convention of the states may be the only hope. The peculiar security of the Constitution, left to us by the founders in the Fifth Article, permits two-thirds of the state legislatures to call a convention for proposing constitutional amendments, and to ratify the Amendments when three-fourths of the states accept the provisions. The people change the Constitution and Congress must accept the new law. It's never been done, but it may be the time, and the only way to correct a mistake of communist theory.

Today's progressive income tax system would disgust the freedom-minded founders. They believed every person should contribute an equal share. Now is the time to return to the true business of government: defense, fair trade and commerce, and fair courts.

Now is the time to restore individual freedom. The common citizen will be freed. No more annual reports. No record keeping. What they earn they keep. Remember the Fifth Article.

Balance the Federal Budget
A Case for Retiring the Debt

GENERATIONS OF AMERICANS have passed their debt to following generations for most of the history of the country. After a century of irresponsible spending, the total debt has reached a size that threatens the freedom and security of the United States. Overspending has been overlooked until it has become a dangerous problem for not only economic security, but also physical safety; the two are difficult to separate. Now, the debt service has become so large that it will soon be necessary to raise taxes or devalue US currency in order to fulfill its obligations. Either of these solutions results with pouring American productivity into sustaining the government, and strips away the opportunity for the private sector to grow and prosper. There would be little left for investment in business or necessary commodities. If the US economy tumbles Americans will experience the same vulnerability that plagued the USSR until it dropped out of the Cold War. It just couldn't keep up, and its security was broken.

The US debt problem is the result of four issues: war, human resources, government growth, and an irresponsible legislature that refuses to accept its responsibility to develop a budget and keep within its limits. The US has remained perpetually embroiled in wars and conflicts in its history, with few intervals of peace. Wars are notorious and large producers of debt; in fact, the country has been left with a huge debt after each one, and seldom has the generation that borrowed the money retired its debt. After the Revolutionary War the new nation was saddled with $75 million in debt. The US debt had grown to $3 billion by 1915, but after World War One the debt ballooned to $25 billion. A similar pattern emerged after World War Two jumping from $42 billion in 1940 to $248 billion by 1945. The debt before Vietnam in 1960 was $290 billion and grew to $576 billion in 1975. Debt numbers became trillions of dollars by 2001 when reported at $5.8 trillion, and it had grown beyond $15 trillion in 2010. Of course, there are other factors included in debt numbers after 1940, such as human resources spending and government growth without limits. Nevertheless, the important indicator of this debt history is that little of it has been retired. Each war operated without complete funding, often a necessity, but the debt remains for today's generation to face.

Following the implementation of the progressive income tax in 1913, the nation began its conversion to a welfare society when it entered the business of providing human resources benefits. For over half its history, the country avoided the idea that its government should provide human resource benefits, but in 1936 it started with income security provided through the Social Security Administration, and was further expanded in 1965 with the addition of medical insurance using Medicare. These benefits are generally considered as earned benefits, that is, most beneficiaries of these plans have paid in to these plans for most of their working lives with the expectation of receiving old age benefits when they can no longer work. A second category has grown enormously in the last fifty years, though, and these are unearned benefits for the recipients. These benefits include education, social services, health care, food stamps, housing assistance, and more. It is not surprising, then, that this surge of human resources spending has vaulted it to the top category of spending in the national budget; it is nearly four times the second highest category of defense spending. Continued spending on human resource benefits beyond the nation's ability to pay for them is perhaps its largest budgetary problem.

The amplified size of the federal government is the nucleus of the country's unending debt situation. Although the expenditures for operating the government are small in comparison to other spending categories, it is the dependence of this governing class of individuals upon the support of program beneficiaries, citizens that is, that makes it virtually impossible for the government to control its spending. The government has grown enormously in proportion to the debt by adding new departments and more people, and by failing to control salaries and benefits until they have become an unfair embarrassment when compared with national workers. The time is past due to return the size of the government to workable levels.

There has been no correction of the debt, or serious effort to contain it, because it is impossible for career politicians to change it. The nature of the Constitution and the political system that has developed under its authority will never serve to correct the country's budget and debt problem; it will never change. The governing class keeps itself in power by giving away a large part of the treasury, and as soon as a career legislator attempts to change it, the career is ended. As a result, Congress cannot be trusted to keep, or even to establish a budget. It can never change, as it exists today.

Change must begin with moral Americans. For one generation to take benefits at the expense of succeeding generations is immoral. The welfare generation of today has been content to collect extra benefits at the expense of future generations by borrowing from China and other sources to support its habit of handouts. Wars of the twenty-first century must similarly be paid off by the current generation. The Middle East Wars should be the current generation's fight for the freedom of their children, and its cost must not be heaped upon them to pick up the tab.

For the sake of the country's future and its morality, it is time to stop the cycle and break the chain. In order to do it, changes in the methods of budgeting and control, and in America's laws will be needed to relieve the burden on career politicians.

THE CORE QUESTION is how much can the United States afford in its budget, and should there be a defined limit?

AMERICAN HISTORY OF BUDGETING AND SPENDING begins with the original purpose and authorization for spending as set down in the Constitution by its writers. When the government commenced business the intent of the people was to collect only enough revenue to support items fixed by the Constitution. The whole purpose of the Constitution was wrapped up in three functions: provide for defense, regulate fair trade and commerce, and establish a court system of fair and equitable laws. Elements of expenditure were confined, then, to defense, communication, commerce standards, administration of federal lands, rules for citizenship, and of course, the federal court system. There were never provisions, nor the intent, to provide for human resources or social programs in the original form of the Constitution.

New purposes were added in the last one hundred years or so. This was accomplished through constitutional interpretation by all branches of government to permit social spending under the Constitution's commerce and welfare clauses. The major human resource addition occurred in 1936 when Social Security was passed into law. It has grown steadily since, with smaller social programs for welfare, food stamps, and so forth; and, of course, the second big addition of Medicare in 1965 with its many facets reaching into American privacy.

Today, then, the national budget provides operating costs for labor, material, facilities, interest, and services. Primary services are defense, infrastructure, and social allotments. The structure of the national budget is divided into receipts and outlays in a manner comparable to a business plan having revenue and expenses.

National receipts are classified as two types: trust funds and federal funds. These are accounting definitions used to segregate the way these receipts are handled. The trust fund term in this sense does not mean the same thing as a private trust where money is held in trust for an owner. Federal trust funds simply identify the receipts for a specific purpose. For example, taxes collected on aviation fuel and airline tickets must be directed to the aviation trust fund solely for aviation use. The largest trust funds are retirement and social insurance funds such as civil service and military retirement, Social Security, Medicare, and unemployment benefits. All taxes collected for these purposes are expressly targeted as trust funds. Conversely, federal funds are defined as all funds not specified by law as trust funds. Generally, all other taxes fall in this category.

The federal budget divides national outlays into twenty functions. These standard categories include expenses, services, and handout programs. They range from national defense and international affairs, agriculture and science, commerce, transportation, and education, to social programs, general government, and interest paid and received. An alternative method for reviewing budget expenditures is used by the Office of Management and Budget (OMB) that reduces the twenty standard functions to five superfunctions. They are classified as defense, human resources, physical resources, net interest, other, and undistributed offsets. Most of these classifications are somewhat self-explanatory. Human resources include payments for the social programs for Social Security, Medicare, Medicaid, income security, education, social services, veterans' benefits, and so forth. Physical resources are primarily directed for energy, natural resources and environment, commerce, transportation, and community development. Expenditures for international affairs, general science, agriculture, and general government are classified as other superfunction outlays. The last category is undistributed offset receipts, which are merely receipts from government sales and other activities. Offset numbers are usually small, and because they generally represent an income stream, they are reflected as a negative amount under outlays.

Studies of the national plan commonly use the viewpoint of percentage of Gross Domestic Product (GDP) to standardize budget numbers for comparison across years. The GDP is a measurement of the economic output, or created wealth, of the country each year. There are various ways of figuring GDP, and the OMB uses its own adjusted figure for comparing budgets across years. In view of the economic doldrums for several years, there is no surprise that the GDP has shown a slowing trend. From 1960 to 1990 the GDP more or less doubled every ten years, but from 1990 to 2000 it grew only about seventy percent, and the ten-year period from 2000 to 2010 only about fifty. Of course, this is the result of economic weakness and high unemployment that have cut revenue.

The source of revenue has changed during the last sixty years, too. Prior to 1913, most government funds were obtained through tariffs and excise taxes, but after the addition of the individual income tax, government began to turn to individual Americans for its funds. By 1960 the leading tax sources were individual and corporate taxes, and individual taxes were roughly double the corporate contributions. By 2000 the individual contribution was 24 times the amount of 1960, but only about twenty percent more in terms of its percentage of GDP. For the same period, corporate taxes were almost ten times the 1960 amount, but the corporate tax as a percentage of GDP dropped by half. The transition to dependence on individual taxes was evident, but it is magnified further when Social Security and Medicare Tax impacts are considered. Naturally there was no Medicare tax in 1960, so the impact was not really felt until later, but by 2010, Social Security and Medicare collections were about equal to individual income taxes paid, each is about six percent of GDP, for that year. The total collections for individual income tax combined with Social Security and Medicare was $1.8 trillion, while corporate tax collections were expected to be only $157 billion. All other tax revenue sources were a tenth to a half percent of GDP each.

Revenues dropped, as a percent of GDP, during the 2000-2010-period, but spending increased to add to the debt problem. Spending grew by about five percent GDP from less than eighteen percent to over twenty-five percent. During this ten-year period, the US was engaged in expensive wars, and social spending was increased to cover unemployment payments, welfare and food stamps benefits, and social insurance obligations. The grand social plans ran into funding problems when the American taxpayer stopped working to support the country's social habit. In response, the federal government continued to add costly plans and to borrow money without limits. Since 2000, it routinely overspent its income by about $200 billion, and in 2010 it was estimated to exceed $1 trillion more than its income. As a result, the American debt mushroomed like a nuclear cloud from $8.3 trillion to over $16 trillion today, and combined with Congressional inaction, it continues to grow.

Predictably, then, the largest source of federal outlays is found in the superfunction definition of human resources. Other payments according to superfunction categories are small in comparison with human resource spending. The estimated expenditures for 2010 were $2.5 trillion for human resources, $719 billion for defense, $214 billion for international affairs, science, agriculture, and general government, $188 billion to pay the net interest due, only $176 billion for physical resources, and about $80 billion in offset receipts income.

Human resource expenditures topping $2.5 trillion were estimated for these services in 2010. When the human resource spending is divided into two categories, earned and unearned, it turns out that outlays for services to individuals that did not pay in are almost as much as the outlays for recipients who did. Paid-in services include not only Social Security and Medicare, but also federal employee retirement payments, veteran benefits and services, and unemployment compensation. Because the Congress continually cites Social Security as the major problem of overspending, the comparison of these benefits with unearned benefits may tell a different story. Payments for Social Security and Medicare remain covered by the trust fund receipts, while at the same time, the payments for unearned benefits are nearly three-quarters of the payments for Social Security and Medicare, but the revenue for unearned benefits must be made up from general funds and loans.

Social spending for programs such as health care services, food and nutrition assistance, housing assistance, supplemental security income, and others is likely the single largest source of the annual deficit. The US is borrowing on its children's credit rating to provide benefits it can't pay for today.

WARS AND SOCIAL ALLOTMENTS for human resources are obviously the first areas to consider in the effort to balance the nation's checkbook. The defense budget can be reduced substantially by bringing service personnel home. As examined previously, the cost for wars are enormous and just keep adding up. The Middle East presence has run over ten years now at huge cost to the country. It is up to this generation to protect the freedom of the United States in the tradition of generations before it, but it is time for this generation to pay for its defense, rather than borrow and pass it on, like it has been done before. The failure of nation building in the Middle East is a tough pill to swallow, but it may be time to finally realize the futility of this effort. The lessons of the British attempts in the region, and the US' own experience with the protracted war in Vietnam should serve as an adequate history lesson for the country's leaders. As long as US countrymen continue to feel the necessity to stabilize one country after another, then this expense will continue growing, and the American people should prepare to contribute a larger portion of its GDP production to this purpose.

In comparing the social allotments for earned benefits with unearned benefits it is reasonable to conclude that Social Security and Medicare really are not the budget problem. These are earned benefits that have been fully funded by their respective taxes since their inception, and remain fully funded today. In contrast, the unearned benefits for welfare and so forth are growing at an even more rapid pace, and today the cost for these benefits is already about three-fourths of the amount paid out for Social Security and Medicare. Here is where the problem lies. The US is spending more for handouts than the working class can afford.

As far as the future of Social Security, the answer may lie in calling the loans on the excess collections that have accumulated for seventy years, but were borrowed from the trust fund and transferred to the federal fund category. A lot of this money was undoubtedly used to pay for the growing unearned benefits for the welfare class.

Increasing the retirement age likely will never work. It simply was a delaying tactic in the 1980s, and will be the same if tried again. The real people hurt when the retirement age is raised are the working poor who have no retirement plan or 401(k). They are required to work longer to receive their social insurance benefit, while their government employee counterparts can retire much earlier, in their 50s if they like, and draw a fat government pension at the expense of the individual who is working toward retirement or Social Security alone. If the retirement age can't stay the same, and if repayment to the program from the treasury won't work, then the whole Social Security system must be reworked at higher cost, or abandoned completely.

THE SIZE OF GOVERNMENT is a smaller, but more insidious source of growing debt. It amounts to about $84 billion a year, but it grows instead of being maintained at a constant level. Every president and every congress seems to judge itself by the amount of legislation it passes with accompanying added programs and benefits. The number of cabinet departments started out with four for President Washington's, but there are more than a dozen now with the irrepressible drive to add. The same can be said for administrative agencies and staff, all growing. Even during the poor economic years starting in 2008, government was adding personnel, although revenues were down, while the rest of the country was cutting jobs to survive. It's a strong indicator of their slow and unwilling ability to adjust to conditions.

The retirement and health care plans for government employees are also out of step with the rest of the country. Adjustments here are needed to bring them more in line with plans available to private citizens. Few companies offer generous retirement plans with early-age retirement possibilities that federal workers receive, and almost no private companies pay a comparable share of health care insurance cost as the American people are required to pay for their federal worker counterparts. If these federal benefits were offset by low regular pay, such that total compensation was in line with US averages, then perhaps these benefits would be warranted. Of course, their pay has increased unchecked for decades, and now their total pay and benefits exceed the compensation of productive workers.

A possible contributor to this imbalance may be the result of the

Congress and Senate including themselves in the benefit system for federal employees. Instead of serving as true representatives of the people, they have been allowed to become little more than federal employees themselves. They accomplished this change in 1946 despite strong objections by the generation of constituents at that time.

A NEGLIGENT CONGRESS IS THE ROOT CAUSE of budget deficits. Of course the executive branch must bear some blame, too, but budgetary controls are the primary responsibility of the Congress, and are its single greatest failure. The Congress offers weak solutions such as raising taxes, making jobs, or offering new plans that ultimately result in more debt. Raising taxes is a poor idea, even if Americans could afford and would approve it. A tax raise is analogous to a company raising prices to cover up its bloated cost structure while still trying to squeeze out a profit. An increase of taxes will do nothing more than hide the current overspending problems, and likely will add more debt as the added revenue is parlayed into additional spending programs instead of paying down the debt.

The government idea to make jobs to generate more revenue is a cruel mistake. The hidden effect is that government only consumes wealth, never builds it. As previously discussed, the US budget consumes up to twenty-five percent of what the country earns. Its effort to add jobs simply adds to the number. There are commonly two methods proposed for adding jobs: tax incentives, or government make-work jobs. The net result of tax incentives for employers to hire workers merely masks the cost of their product and passes it on to the taxpaying public in the form of taxes. A properly sized company will inflate its costs if it hires personnel it doesn't need; it would be similar to paying $1,000 at 20% off for something unneeded. In reality, $1,000 was wasted.

Adam Smith, often considered the father of economics, explained over two hundred years ago that no government regulation or manipulation of commerce can increase real job demand beyond the strong value that leads to more sales requiring more individuals to keep up with demand. Until the federal government of today is ready and willing to establish a concrete plan to cut government size and expense, it will merely continue with its pattern of new plans and gimmicks until the final disaster.

THE CONCLUSION IS STAGGERING. The net result is that debt numbers are growing, the human resources unearned benefits are the main source of annual deficits, and the Congress is unwilling to meet its responsibility of fiscal stewardship entrusted to it by common citizens. The deficit grows over $1 trillion each year, and the only response is to raise the debt ceiling, while continuing to borrow, predominately from China, for the welfare payout. Welfare recipients are receiving benefits today at the expense of the next generation, which will be forced to suffer the consequences of the debt.

Realistically, there are only two choices for correcting the debt problem: increase taxes or reduce outlays. Increasing taxes can occur by raising individual rates, or by adding more taxpayers as a result of improved national productivity. Increasing the individual tax rate in order to cover the huge human resource and defense shortfall is not likely to be popular with public opinion. There is a limit for taxpayers, and it may have been reached.

Reducing outlays in a long-term plan to reduce the debt is the only sensible way to correct the problem. For any private business faced with a similar problem, the solution would be both short-term and long-term corrective action to be implemented in an organized and controlled program. The national debt is the result of imprudent stewardship beyond the ways and means of the country for decades; similarly, it will require a long time to correct. There are decades-old promises made to individuals and businesses that must not be recklessly cancelled. It may take a decade or more to put the country on the right path, but it is better than total default on promises and debts.

Four parts to an organized plan include fixed budget levels, reduced size of government, routine government cost reductions, and new and unbending legislation to control and remove the opportunity for Congress to waiver from its responsibility.

Fixed budget limits are required for total revenue intake and for each of the outlay functions. Limits may be set as a percentage of the GDP or other suitable measure of national production. For example, if eighteen percent of GDP were selected as the revenue limit, then no more than that would be available to the government. For a GDP of $15 trillion, the eighteen-percent maximum would be $2.7 trillion.

Similar restrictions would apply to spending. A percentage for each outlay function, such as defense, human resources, and so forth would be the limit of spending. If the limit for unearned human resources is forty percent of revenue, then the limit on $2.7 trillion would be $1.1 trillion, and payouts must be adjusted to meet these requirements. Americans can grasp the idea that borrowing cannot continue to be the way of providing nonproductive benefits such as welfare.

Fixed-budget legislation should include a set amount to retire the debt. A long-term goal for becoming debt free would be used to establish an estimated percentage of GDP that will be used to pay down the debt. In addition, there must be emergency provisions, such as war defense, that would allow the country to borrow for defense if necessary. Naturally, a payback period would be required for any war debt. Under fixed-budget legislation, the size of government would be subject to the size of the GDP. When GDP is low, government must be cut.

The second element of correcting the debt involves an all out review and correction of the size of government. It too should include short- and long-term fixes. An immediate reduction in force of ten percent should be implemented. Although it will likely have a minimal effect on the debt, seldom does an organization continue with unrestrained personnel growth for as long as the federal government has, without a huge buildup of waste. Probably much more than ten percent can be offset, but an immediate cut should be used to sound the depth. In the longer term the entire size of government should be compared with the economy and revenue receipts in order to determine the reasonable size of government in comparison with the size of business it does. It may be necessary to eliminate whole departments. Those with poor performance records, such as the Department of Education, should be abolished.

In reviewing government size and operations, the pay, retirement, and health benefits of federal workers should be equalized with national averages. With the advent of 401(k) retirement plans, many corporations have shifted the responsibility for retirement planning to the individual. The new idea is that retiree income should come from three sources: a small company benefit, Social Security benefits, and personal savings like the 401(k). Company paid pension plans are small, or nonexistent today, so workers are expected to provide for themselves. It's a cost reduction strategy that should carry to the government sector. A structured plan to keep pay and benefits at national averages should be used to control unreasonable wage creep. Each year the comparison should be made with national averages and then required by law to be adjusted to meet the national average.

The national government has cost reduction plans, but they are ineffective. Debt reduction legislation should add teeth to their plans requiring tangible, measurable, reductions in operating costs. It should include a provision to eliminate congressionally directed spending, or earmarks. Although the waste eliminated by such a law will not retire the debt, it will contribute to reducing the burgeoning human resources hunger. If nothing more, eliminating earmarks will remove a burr from under the saddle of most Americans.

Fixed-budget legislation must be strong, iron clad, unbending. In today's political environment, with today's system of government, it is unlikely that career politicians will ever think about, much less engage, in implementing hard legislation to reduce the debt and size of government. They fear for their jobs, and they should. It would be political suicide for anyone brave enough to suggest it.

Honestly, there is likely only one solution that can provide a rigid law to control collections and spending, and that would be a constitutional amendment, a balanced budget amendment. Thomas Jefferson sensed this problem during the country's infancy and wrote that he wished for a balanced budget amendment. It would free the career politician from the burden of suggesting cuts in benefits, because it would be written into the law of the people, and legislators take an oath to follow the Constitution. They would have no choice.

It would take a true and courageous patriot to suggest and follow through with budget changes. John Kennedy's book, *Profiles In Courage*, suggest there have been strong individuals in the past, and there may be in the future. If not, perhaps a common citizen will initiate a movement for a Constitutional Convention of the States to consider the change that would be at the hands of the people.

Human Resource Spending
A Case for Adjustment

HUMAN RESOURCE SPENDING by the federal government is a somewhat new concept in American history. Also known as entitlement spending, the founders of the country never envisioned it, and there were no direct provisions for it in the Constitution. In fact, the majority of early Americans did not view human resource spending as a responsibility of the federal government at all.

Today, entitlement spending on human resources has a long history and is firmly entrenched into American society. It is so enrooted that the line between unalienable and vested rights has become blurred in the minds of both citizens and federal officials. The country's founders were seeking protection of unalienable rights; these are the natural birthrights that morally cannot be taken away. All freeborn citizens have the personal right to freedom of thoughts, speech, their conscience, and so forth. Vested rights are granted by government statute. These statutory rights are completely reversible and can be revoked by a government at any time. Examples of vested rights include food, clothing, housing, and others.

When federal representatives speak of people's rights to health care, for example, they are referring to a vested, statutory right. Unfortunately, in their zeal to push for or against one of these rights, they fail to make the distinction, or worse, it smudges their personal ability to make the distinction. The importance of the distinction is that only unalienable rights are the gift of nature that no one can dispute, while vested rights exist in the human mind and not every citizen agrees that they are truly rights.

Human resource spending has grown to enormous proportions and is the largest element of the federal budget. It includes both social insurance and welfare programs. This spending is often segregated into two categories: earned and unearned entitlements. Earned entitlements refers to programs where the recipients have a record of contributions to a trust fund for part or all of their working lives. The Social Security and Medicare programs fall into this category. It is a form of social insurance making it feasible for people to pay for insurance when they are young and able to work and be assured of receiving benefits when they are older and no longer working. Some people will contribute more than they receive in return, and others less, but this is common for many forms of insurance. The most common earned benefits paid from the federal budget are Social Security, Medicare, federal employee retirement plans, veterans' benefits and services, and unemployment compensation.

Conversely, unearned benefits include welfare programs such as food stamps, housing assistance, health care, and education assistance. Virtually none of these program recipients have paid into the system, and there is no limit to how much the nation must commit to those who qualify. As a result, unearned entitlement spending has grown until it almost equals Social Security and Medicare expenditures.

The major social insurance plans are Social Security and Medicare, and both programs are under the direction of the Social Security Administration (SSA). The Social Security program is about seventy-five years old, and for about half of that time Americans have been warned that the SSA may be unable to meet its commitments in the future. Medicare is approaching fifty years of operation, and the similar warning from federal officials is that money may run out for it too, if something isn't changed.

In reality, the Social Security Trust Fund is one of the largest holders of US Treasury debt. Of course, China and Japan are huge lenders to the American lifestyle, but the Social Security Trust Fund loans amounts of similar magnitude. Nevertheless, federal officials insist that incoming payments and the amount in reserve will be used up if something isn't done.

The common response from Congress is to increase the retirement age. Presumably the original program didn't plan on people living so long with so many complicated diseases and expensive treatments. Increasing the minimum age was tried once before in the eighties, and it was touted as a fix for the program. They missed like a bad weather forecast, and now the nation is faced with a recurring problem. Not only is it unlikely to be a permanent fix, but also it is unfair to the working poor who have no type of private retirement plan or savings. These folks will be stuck working and paying longer for less benefit than government counterparts that may retire in their fifties and pay nothing more into the system.

Welfare programs for beneficiaries that have not paid-in, or invested in their relief plans, have mushroomed like an atomic bomb cloud; suddenly the nation has been saddled with an overwhelming demand for human resource spending that exceeds its tax receipts and its ability to pay, and the congressional answer for the dilemma has been to borrow ever increasing amounts. The nation borrows from foreign sources in order to meet its welfare promises, and there are no boundaries or ceiling to control it. Now, the US spends nearly as much on unearned benefits as it does for Social Security and Medicare.

Total human resource spending has become the largest part of the American budget. The estimates for 2010 expected about sixty-seven percent of total outlays would be for human resource programs. The breakdown of human resource spending was about forty-three percent for earned benefits, with the Social Security and Medicare portion accounting for about thirty-two percent of the total budget. Comparatively, spending on unearned benefits was about twenty-four percent of the total national spending budget.

With two-thirds of the budget committed to human resources, the remaining third was tagged for true taxpayer services: nineteen percent for defense, and about five percent each for physical resources, interest on the debt, and other categories. Physical resources can include important parts of building American infrastructure for energy, transportation, commerce, and community development. The space program and other technology development programs, agriculture, international affairs, and government administration receive similarly small funding amounts. These budget elements make up a part of the five percent total for other spending.

The important point when comparing budget spending is that precious few American tax dollars are spent on defense, commerce, courts, or infrastructure. Taxpayer contributions are largely given away, some to those who have paid-in for a return, and boundless amounts for individuals who never paid-in. Worse, the country borrows the money it gives away.

Clearly, changes are necessary for both paid-in and not paid-in programs in order to remain within the limits of national tax revenue.

THE CORE QUESTION for modern Americans is whether human resource programs should be limited, and if so what adjustments should be made?

THE VIEWS OF SOCIETY have changed since the country was founded. It has evolved from a society in its earliest days that insisted on little involvement by a small federal government in private lives, to a huge federal government that seeks to manipulate virtually every phase of privacy and gives aid to those who qualify according to legislative standards. The majority of folks in Thomas Jefferson's generation believed charity was not the business of government. It was the view that charity should remain in the hands of the states and local citizens. In fact, federal spending for charity or human resources was commonly viewed as unconstitutional, because there was no direct language that authorized it. This conviction remained firm in American society for fifty years or more. In the early nineteenth century, as late as the 1830s, the country continued to oppose human resource spending by the federal government. Local citizens believed their tax dollars were not sent to Washington to give away to others.

After its first one hundred years of existence, the United States began to change. Perhaps it was the change of times, or the sensational theories of communism, or a combination of influences; whatever it was, the country began to accept the ideas of relief and taxing the rich. A major breakthrough of this idea occurred around 1913 when the Sixteenth Amendment to the Constitution was ratified to permit unequal taxation that would require citizens with higher incomes to support a larger portion of the nation's income. It was the beginning of the idea of taking from the wealthy to give to the less fortunate.

The next big step, of course, was approval of the Social Security and welfare plans in 1935. It was the beginning of the explosion of earned and unearned programs in the twentieth century. This idea of federal spending for human resources was born through clever and imaginative interpretation of the Constitution. An elementary school student can read the Constitution and realize there is no direct federal authorization to give away tax money to individual citizens. By working together, though, segments of all branches of government were able to read between the lines. Their interpretation of the general welfare, commerce, and implied powers clauses was used to advance their power to tax one group of citizens to support another. In simple terms, the claim was that human resources spending would be for the general welfare of all Americans, that it was merely exercising its authorization to regulate commerce, and to make all laws that were necessary and proper for executing these powers. The floodgates were cracked, but not wide open.

The Old Age, Survivors, and Disability Insurance Act of 1935, and its amendments, established several social welfare and social insurance plans. The Social Security program was introduced as a completely voluntary program, and enrollees were issued a card; curiously, this card was not to be used as an ID, and early cards were marked, "Not for Identification." Eventually, of course, both the provisions for voluntary participation and the prohibition of use as an ID were reversed about thirty years ago. Now, the use of the Social Security Number for identification is almost universal, and one of the major users of it is the Internal Revenue Service. Originally the benefits received by retired beneficiaries were not taxed as income, but in 1984, as part of the effort to save the system from future insolvency, the retirement age was raised, and for high-income retirees, a portion of their Social Security became taxable.

Social Security was a great deal for those who got into the program early when the ratio of contributors to beneficiaries was high. The first beneficiary was Ida Fuller. She paid about forty-four dollars in Social Security taxes and collected almost $21,000 in benefits before her death. As late as 1950 it was reported that there were sixteen workers paying taxes to support each retiree, but today there are only three.

Despite the projected problems in covering Social Security payments, a government consumed with handing out vested rights charged headlong into the Medicare plan of 1966. It was a substantial increase of the human resource drain on the treasury. Medicare was created under a title of the Social Security Act to provide health insurance for people aged at least sixty-five. During its operation, there have been several changes to Medicare to further expand it to include benefits for speech, physical therapy, and more. Eventually, the Congress continued to add to the original expense by extending eligibility to younger people with permanent disabilities who receive disability payments.

These are the primary earned benefits programs. The actions of 1935 also started the flow of unearned benefits. The first food stamp program followed it shortly to appropriate federal funds from 1939 to 1943. Some acclaimed food stamps as a responsible step toward wise use of agricultural abundance. In the meantime, the debt continued to grow. As of 2013 more than fifteen percent of the US population receives food assistance.

Today, there are government payments for a suite of welfare benefits. These are usually means-tested benefits to identify the degree of need for each case. It includes education, training, and employment and social services. There are health care services such as Medicaid, housing assistance for needy families, and payments for pregnant women. Supplemental Security Income has become a major source of support for low-income disabled adults, and severely disabled children. As a result of the number of annual applications, topping 650,000 a year, the US administrative courts have become the largest US court system.

A new addition to government assistance plans is the Patient Protection and Affordable Care Act of 2010 that will subsidize health care insurance benefits. It makes the fourth large step of the federal government into the business of human resources. Citizens will be required to procure personal health insurance. Those who refuse will pay a fine at the tax desk when they file their annual tax return. Those who cannot afford the health insurance premium will receive an assistance payment from federal and state sources. If the assistance is too much or too little, the recipients will be required to reconcile an adjustment on their tax returns.

The transformation of American society is remarkable, from its beginning as a nation of independent citizens to a country of victims on the dole. Because there have been no limits on the amount of handouts, the human resources commitment has grown beyond all imaginable proportions. From virtually no benefits to over $2 trillion a year for dozens of programs, human resource spending spans numerous departments of government. Once an individual has been drawn into dependence on public assistance it is easy to see how the distinction between vested and unalienable rights has been blurred.

SOCIAL SECURITY REVISIONS have been discussed for decades. Officials claim spending must be held within limits of income, or the program will bust. There have been some changes as discussed in the history of the program, but it remains a hot topic that apparently remains without a definitive fix. It frightens seniors, and near seniors, that have nowhere else to turn after they are too old to work, and a cloud of desperation hangs over very young workers as they conclude from dreary reports that nothing will be available to them when they reach retirement age. It is a terribly mismanaged program with little emphasis from national legislators to correct it.

The system is a stand-alone program that is built upon its own dedicated revenue sources. Both workers and employers pay into the Social Security Trust Fund through payroll taxes that amount to 12.4 percent of individual earnings. Money collected for the trust fund is sent to the US Treasury where the Treasury Department borrows the money by selling Treasury notes to the Social Security Trust Fund. Payments into the fund generally have exceeded payouts to beneficiaries during its history, and today there is a surplus of around $2.7 trillion in the form of these Treasury notes. When the Social Security Administration makes its payments to beneficiaries, it redeems enough Treasury notes to meet its obligations. Of course, the federal government operates in the red with a debt exceeding $16 trillion, so it must issue more Treasury notes to offset the monthly redemption by the Social Security Administration.

Management of Social Security is conflicted. Among its senior trustees are the Secretary of the Treasury, Secretary of Health and Human Services, Secretary of Labor, and the Commissioner of the Social Security Administration. These individuals must balance their loyalties to the president, other welfare programs, and to the earned-benefits enrollees of the Social Security program. These other departments are somewhat tied to the income of the Social Security Trust Fund, and they compete for the ability to borrow against it to finance other elements of government agenda.

Although Social Security payments are distributed to beneficiaries who receive earned benefits, in reality the benefit amounts are based on income earned during the working life of each beneficiary. It is a needs-based system of graduated payments. Low-income workers receive a larger replacement percentage of their working income than workers at the top of the income scale. The highest-income worker receives a higher dollar amount from Social Security, but it is not proportional to the difference in contribution amounts paid in by the lowest-income employee. Recipients who qualify for the top level of Social Security benefits receive about twenty-six percent of their pre-retirement income, while those at the minimum level can receive benefits that are as much as ninety-four percent of their qualifying working income.

Despite its history of operating with a surplus, accounting specialists report that this will be reversed in the not-to-distant future. Soon, it is projected, payouts will exceed receipts and the surplus in the trust fund will be exhausted. Now is the time, they warn, to correct the situation, before it is altogether too late. The majority of ideas begin by increasing the retirement age in order to delay payouts. The problem with this solution is that it is completely unfair to workers with no retirement plan. Workers without pensions who earned high incomes for most of their careers may or may not have some sort of savings to help, but the higher age requirement will be most cruel to the low-income employee with no savings. These workers will be required to work even longer to meet higher age requirements, while their fortunate fellow citizens, with generous retirement plans to fall back on, may not only receive more but also begin retirement much earlier.

Higher retirement ages appears to be a simple solution, but it didn't work thirty years ago, and it's likely to resurface in the future if attempted again. Either the program must be adequately funded, or it should be phased out.

MEDICARE WAS ADDED to the list of human resources administered by the federal government in 1965. It is a defined-benefit plan that guarantees access to health insurance for people when they reach age sixty-five, and for younger people with disabilities. There are special allowances to admit people to the program that have contracted specific disabling diseases. The idea is to spread the financial risk of the insurance across society to protect everyone.

Like all human resources plans before it, the Medicare program has been expanded through the years. Science and medicine have advanced since 1965 such that life expectancy has increased as well. As a result, Medicare was expanded to add more services for the later stages of life and hospice benefits. Today the program provides health care to more than forty million elderly recipients and eight million younger, but disabled.

Medicare benefits are somewhat graduated, also. It is established in the form of the premium amount for the part B medical coverage for doctors and other health care needs. Every Medicare recipient pays an insurance premium for this basic coverage, but it differs according to the income range of the insured. Individuals who report income above a certain amount on their income tax return from two years ago may have to pay an extra charge added to the standard premium. There are five premium graduations by income, and in 2013 it ranged from $104.90 per month to $335.70 per month. Often these are the same folks who paid much more in Medicare taxes when they were working, and then if their retirement income is similarly high, they will continue to pay higher premiums, regardless of their health. Other situations can land Medicare recipients in a high premium bracket for a year or more. Folks who cash an annuity or savings plan may be faced with a high income for a year or more. The same thing may happen to individuals who have saved a lifetime in their IRA, and then must withdraw required minimum distributions after age seventy. The reward for these savers is higher total income taxes, higher taxes on their Social Security, and a higher Medicare insurance premium.

Like Social Security, the Medicare program is a stand-alone program that operates on its own revenue stream collected from employees and employers. Also like Social Security, it is reported that costs will soon outpace collections and the program will run out of money. Both of the great human resource creations of the twentieth century have not been modified for the times, and as a result are in danger of default; that is, if the predictions of economic forecasters are a suitable crystal ball.

UNEARNED ENTITLEMENTS are probably the fastest growing segment of the human resources outlays by the federal government. These are the benefits without boundaries that are received by individuals who have not contributed eligibility premiums or taxes. Generally the recipients are those individuals who are unable to work, or who do not choose to work. Many of these folks have established a way of life around government benefits that may extend across three or more generations. Folks who have elected government subsistence have grown to view it as an American vested right.

They view their citizenship as a right to food relief, housing help, free medical coverage, a spending allowance, and in some cases today, a free cell phone with a stipend for government-paid connection minutes. Commonly called welfare, unearned entitlements usually refers to means-tested cash and non-cash benefits. The possibilities are staggering. Some of the major benefits are Temporary Assistance for Needy Families (TANF), the Special Supplemental Nutrition Program for Women, Infants, and Children (WIC), the Supplemental Nutritional Assistance Program (SNAP), Medicaid, and now the new Patient Protection and Affordable Care Act (PPAC). Payments and benefits of these programs are generally based upon poverty level figures. In 2013 the poverty level for an individual was set at $11,490, and a family of four at $23,550.

The TANF program, or Temporary Assistance for Needy Families began in 1997 and is actually a replacement for two preceding programs. It replaced Aid to Families with Dependent Children (AFDC), which was created by the Social Security Act in1935, and originally called Aid to Dependent Children. Like all aid programs, it grew. From a minor part of the social security system to a primary form of welfare, it was administered by the states with federal funding. It was replaced by TANF, which carried more restrictions, because the earlier AFDC plan was criticized as encouraging single mothers of non-marital births to stay at home, rather than seeking employment. The aim of TANF is to get people off assistance and into the workplace by limiting benefits to a maximum of sixty months per lifetime, depending upon the policies of individual states.

While the TANF program is administered by the Department of Health and Human Services, many of the food assistance plans are Department of Agriculture programs. The Special Supplemental Nutrition Program for Women, Infants, and Children (WIC) is an Ag Department program to help low-income pregnant women, breastfeeding women, and children under five. Income limits for recipients is 185% of the US poverty guidelines, or about $28,684 a year for two people, and over fifty percent of all infants receive WIC benefits. It was started around 1969 on the recommendation of a group of clinical doctors that reported various ailments among pregnant women caused by lack of food. In order to qualify for WIC, a pregnant woman or mother must have specific nutritional needs and meet other specific criteria.

One of the best-known programs by Americans is the food stamp program, more formally known as the Supplemental

Nutritional Assistance Program (SNAP). Following the first food stamp program that ran from 1939 to 1943, the current program kicked off in 1964. The needs-based plan is based primarily on income and resources of the recipient. Gross income is limited to 130 percent of the poverty line. In 2013, a single person earning less than $14,937 would be eligible, and so would a family of four bringing in less than $30,615. There are additional restrictions on household assets, which may not exceed $2,000 unless someone is disabled. Benefits for one person exceed $2,000 per year and a family of four can generally expect to receive about $7,500 for a full year. This food program is also administered by the Department of Agriculture, which reports that roughly 48 million Americans received food stamps in 2013.

Health care assistance is provided for individuals with low-income resources by the Medicaid program. It is a means-tested plan, too, which is jointly funded by state and federal governments. Although states are not required to participate in the plan, each does and manages its plan and eligibility requirements. The federal government establishes minimum eligibility guidelines, but states may increase them.

The Medicaid program is extensive, covering children, pregnant women, low-income adults, disabled adults, and low-income seniors. Children from low-income families are prime recipients, and the program provides health coverage to over 31 million children. Medicaid also furnishes health coverage to low-income parents and pregnant women. Forty percent of all US births include Medicare benefits from prenatal care through labor and delivery, and for sixty days afterward. Disabled adults may receive Medicaid assistance, and almost 9 million received health coverage in 2013. Low-income seniors who are covered by Medicare but are unable to afford their part of Medicare payments may have the difference made up by Medicaid. Nearly five million seniors received this Medicaid benefit this year.

Now a new source of Medicaid health care assistance begins in 2014, authorized by the Patient Protection and Affordable Care Act of 2010. It offers assistance on health insurance premiums for citizens within poverty-line guidelines. According to family size and income level, there will be a maximum out-of-pocket payment for health insurance. A single individual earning less than 133% of the poverty level, $15,281 annually, would not have to pay more than $288 per year for health insurance. If the same person earned four times the poverty level, $45,960, then the maximum premium would be $4,115 a year. A family of four below 133 percent of the poverty level, $31,321, will be expected to pay no more than $587 a year for their family health coverage.

Naturally this new plan has caused an uproar in the country, especially because it was passed quickly by a Congress that did not understand it, and because it forces Americans to report to the Internal Revenue Service that they have health care insurance, and to pay a tax penalty if they don't have the required coverage. If the massive PPAC plan follows the track record of the human resource programs that have preceded it, then it is entirely likely that it will not be adequately funded.

THE CONCLUSION IS SIMPLE; adjustments to human resource spending are necessary if the country hopes to reduce its debt and dependence on foreign loans. Adjustments are needed for both earned and unearned benefits plans and should be considered independently. Stand-alone plans, such as Social Security and Medicare must be adequately funded to meet the lifetime promises made when involuntary taxes are collected from citizens. Payout ceilings are needed for welfare programs that are paid for with taxes from US workers and loans from foreign nations.

Of course the problems with all of America's human resource programs are caused by decades of neglect at the Congressional level. Similarly, the repairs to these programs will require a decade or more to complete. Social Security and Medicare modifications should include changes to funding limits, modification of eligibility rules, and revision of accounting methods for borrowing from the trust funds. Unearned welfare benefits should be contained by maximum spending limits.

First is what the country should not do to fix Social Security, unless there are equal changes among society. Do not increase the retirement age eligibility for low-income workers. Instead of moving to increase the retirement age, it should be held in similar proportion to the plan for federal employees. If federal employees are to be eligible for early retirement, so should be Social Security beneficiaries. The Social Security plan is likely the only plan available for low-income workers. It is unreasonable to expect these individuals to work longer than other citizens to earn the benefits of lifetime payments.

An immediate adjustment to the Social Security plan that could put it on solid ground for several more decades is to lift the ceiling on income subject to Social Security taxes. If all earnings were subject to the payroll tax, but the base for figuring benefits kept the same, then the threat of running out of money will be pushed back several decades, if not permanently. High-income workers and employers won't like it, because it will add considerably to the cost structure of their businesses.

An additional change would be to extend the needs basis of paying out Social Security benefits. Already, the current benefit formula replaces a much higher percentage of the working-pay of low-income workers than it does for the higher-income worker. It isn't a much larger step to eliminate it altogether for those fortunate enough to have high returns from personal pension plans. This would affect individuals that already receive generous pensions that replace a high percentage of their pre-retirement income. Their Social Security benefit would be reduced in proportion to the amount of working pay that is replaced by pension income. For example, individuals receiving pension payments that exceed fifty percent of their working income may begin to see a phase out of a portion of their Social Security income. Folks receiving pensions with high replacement income percentages would not receive Social Security payments at all. There are folks who receive private or government pensions that amount to eighty percent or more of what they earned while they worked, and they collect Social Security benefits, too. It can be argued that they don't need the additional Social Security income, and should not be eligible to receive it.

Another modification using the means-testing method for authorizing Social Security payments would be to exclude high-income individuals from receiving benefits. Of course it is unfair, but it is no less unfair than requiring all taxpayers to contribute for unearned benefits, such as food stamps, that they will likely never receive, either. People earning millions a year simply do not need a Social Security supplement. A retired Congressman drawing over $150,000 a year in retirement benefits should not be eligible for another $20,000 from Social Security. The payout, then, becomes needs-based for those who have little or no pension and little income from savings.

Finally, accounting changes are needed to protect the Social Security reserve. The method of issuing bonds on tax receipts and sweeping them into the general fund makes the trust fund a fragile line on the paper entry. The Social Security Trust Fund should be set up with reserve and funding limits that are no different than any other pension plan. Investing in US bonds is a sensible idea, but not without limits. There should be a fixed reserve that is large enough to fund the payouts according to actuarial rules, but not so large as to tempt abuse. Tax payments should be adjusted according to the reserve amount. If the reserve grows too large the tax rate should be reduced, and vice versa. The days of indiscriminate borrowing to feed the welfare habit must end.

If hard adjustments such as described are too expensive, or too difficult for society to bear, then it should face the fact that it can't really afford it. The debt of these benefits is simply being piled onto the next generation. This history of the US debt is an inescapable record of the effects of human resource programs. If it is too much, then it is time to admit the plan is not workable and should be eliminated altogether.

Revisions to Medicare can parallel steps to secure Social Security retirement benefits, but it should include revisions to national health care rules, too. Health care insurance should be deregulated to permit portability and to allow all plans to be available to all individuals throughout the country. Instead of depending upon an employer to provide health care coverage and then losing it when moving to another type of employment, all Americans should have an equal opportunity to purchase insurance and carry it with them throughout their working lives. Instead of being excluded by age and infirmity after retirement, a worker would have a long history of affordable payments that would fund medical payments throughout the needs of a lifetime. It would be financed the same way as cash benefits for retirement. Contributions would be paid while at work when least burdensome, with protection furnished in retirement with reduced premiums or no premiums at all.

As long as the country relies on the Medicare plan to cover the medical expenses of the elderly, it must be adequately funded. The same difficult adjustments that were suggested for Social Security should be applied to the Medicare program. The current funding level is 2.9 percent, 1.45 percent each for employee and employer. If this is inadequate, as is commonly suggested by the Congress, then it must be increased to maintain the promise of the last fifty years made to the public. Similarly, the need-basis must be modified to disqualify high-income applicants. It can be argued that folks earning above $300,000 or so during retirement can afford their own insurance, and should be ineligible for the benefits.

Social insurance has shifted away from personal responsibility to a view that it is an entitlement to be provided at others' expense. The Social Security and Medicare plans, and all earned benefits plans, must be fully funded by the recipients. The welfare factor should be replaced by the responsibility factor where feasible.

Unearned entitlement spending is a different problem. These are unbounded plans with no ceiling on the amount spent. The Congress may try to budget an amount to be spent for human resources, but if more people demand benefits than expected, the country simply borrows the money to give away. A parable would be a benevolent soul who uses a credit card to donate $100,000 a year to charity while earning only $20,000 a year. The debt piles up, but the philanthropist continues to borrow against the credit limit until there is no hope and the good-hearted, but irresponsible, contributor becomes a candidate for charity, too. Such is the situation for the United States. The folks who urge beneficial programs mean well, but it has become so large that the wealth-producing workers of America can no longer afford it. As a result, the total debt is piled onto the shoulders of future generations. The people who receive unearned benefits not only live at the expense of their fellow citizens, but at the expense of the American youth and the unborn. It will be their problem to solve.

It has been a seventy-five year spending frenzy for America involving social insurance and unearned welfare. Every program has grown. New programs are added almost daily. The Congress judges the effectiveness of its activity on how many new programs are created to add to the suite of entitlements. Now it is just about at the breaking point, and it is time for Americans to decide how much is affordable.

Boundaries are needed. Unearned benefits should be capped two ways: a limit on the amount of the federal budget that can spent for unearned benefits; and, a credit ceiling to restrict the amount that can be borrowed for unearned payouts. The overall goal should be no borrowing to fund human resources.

Spending limits could be tied to a percentage of the national budget, to the Gross Domestic Product, or to other suitable means of establishing a budgeted maximum payout. If actual expenditures exceed limits, then unearned benefits should be reduced to maintain budget restraints. In order to meet extraordinary or crisis demands, then borrowing may be authorized within predetermined set limits. The combination of spending and borrowing limits would establish the country's ability, or willingness, to pay for unearned human resources.

All borrowing for human resources must be repaid during the lifespan of the generation of citizens that authorize it. Automatic tax increases must be required to retire the debts of deficit spending for human resources. If the debt reaches a given level, then taxes must be increased to pay it off. It is past time for leaving the excesses of one generation for future citizens to face. If the country can't afford it, it shouldn't commit to it.

Executive Power
A Case for Boundaries

THE EXECUTIVE BRANCH has grown with unchecked power for the last one hundred years until it has become a threat to replace the power of the people to self-govern. It is the direct result of constitutional interpretation that has infected all branches of the US government. Instead of adhering to the plain language of the Constitution, and then asking the people openly when changes are needed to support programs that do not comply with the Constitution, government officials often ignore the Constitution altogether, or seek to find obscure meaning in its words to fit their personal plans. A good example is the Social Security system and the maneuvering around the Constitution to justify it by claiming it falls within the powers of the general welfare clause (Article I, Section 8, Clause 1) and the commerce clause (Article I, Section 8, Clause 3). Of course it doesn't, and the nation remains divided over it to this day. A constitutional amendment to add social insurance to the powers of government was the upfront method intended by the originators of the national contract.

This is but one example. Long before Social Security, the executive branch was busy with its own brand of seizing power for its purpose. The legislative branch has permitted it to some extent, by delegating a large portion of its lawmaking power to the executive branch. Congress uses the expedient of delegated legislation to authorize the various executive agencies to develop details based upon the broad principles of a Congressional law. An example is rulemaking by the Internal Revenue Service based upon Congressional tax provisions. The Congress has developed national programs in huge numbers and complexity until it has lost a fair amount of its ability to check the power of the Executive branch. Its primary recourse is to refuse to fund the provisions of an executive order, but the president can veto funding limitations, and the veto is exceptionally difficult to override. Now, the executive branch is the largest lawmaking arm of the government, despite the clear lawmaking assignment made to the Congress by the Constitution. This unbalance threatens to replace the rule of the people with board rule by an elite few.

The growth of executive power is the result of laws issued by executive orders, through special advisors, and by executive agencies. Theodore Roosevelt expanded executive orders enormously at the turn of the century as he made his own orders without regard for the Constitution. The growth in size and scope of the Office of the President has developed into a group of more than thirty special advisors employing over 400 people. These groups are busy setting policy and making new rules outside the purview of Congress. The presidential cabinet and executive agencies have matched the phenomenal growth of the Executive Office of the President, and these agencies are churning out rules, regulations, and punishments as a matter of routine business.

The danger of too much power in one branch of government has developed. The executive branch is now larger than the people's house. Checks and balances are threatened. Laws are being made without accountability to the people. The rule of self-government is jeopardized, and actions are needed to reverse it.

THE CORE QUESTION is whether the lawmaking authority of the executive branch and its agencies should be restricted or left as a second lawmaking branch without accountability to the people of the country?

HISTORICALLY THE UNITED STATES was established as a government of Rule of the People, as opposed to Board Rule. People's rule refers to laws formed by self-governing people and implemented through common law. These are laws from the people up to the government. Common laws are the result of the common law jury system, and the founders intended it as the ultimate defense against people being overpowered by the government. Conversely, board rules are formed by a central authority, such as the executive agencies, and become laws from the government down to the people. An elite few decide laws, enforcement methods, and punishment. All executive branch power is board rule. Examples are the Environmental Protection Agency (EPA), Internal Revenue Service (IRS), Occupational Safety and Health Administration (OSHA), Health & Human Services (HHS), and others.

For most of these executive rule makers there is no direct

accountability to the people; instead, they operate under the umbrella of designated legislation authorized by acts of Congress. The president is elected, and the Senate approves Cabinet officers, but many special advisors and their assistants work without approval by the people, and they routinely author laws, without Congressional approval, and impose them on the citizens of the country. It's board rule without representation.

Every president wrestles with what executive acts are constitutional. In their zeal to accomplish their party's goals for the country, they often want to do things outside the power granted to them by the Constitution. In fact, Article II defines executive power, and it is limited to military authority, authorization to make treaties and appoint Supreme Court justices, appoint officers according to responsibility delegated by Congress, and to appoint officers when the Senate is vacant. The use of executive orders spawned from the same Second Article. It is vaguely interpreted from the wording of the first sentence of the First Clause of the First Section that reads, "The executive power shall be vested in a President of the United States of America," and it is further stretched by the wording in the Third Section that in part reads, "he shall take care that the laws be faithfully executed." Alternatively, the Tenth Amendment in the Bill of Rights protects the people with its statement that powers not delegated by the Constitution are reserved to the people. That is, if it isn't stated in the Constitution as a specific power, it isn't authorized.

Many presidents have perverted their power believing they knew what was best for the country, whether or not the people agreed with them. Executive orders are a prime example of this abuse. All presidents have used executive orders. They were originally used to control the activities of the executive staff. George Washington used the executive order, but the practice of numbering them wasn't started until 1907. The numbering was a result of Theodore Roosevelt's decision to test the powers of executive orders. Roosevelt openly stated that he believed the president could do anything not forbidden by the Constitution. He should have read the Bill of Rights. Contrast his statement to James Madison's explanation that the federal government is limited to doing only what the Constitution grants. It wouldn't matter, though, Roosevelt dangerously believed his agenda was best for America, and he intended to implement it using executive orders despite the Constitution. The result was astounding. Four years prior to Roosevelt's service as president, Grover Cleveland issued 71 executive orders. In his challenge for authority, Theodore Roosevelt stepped it up to 1,006. Theodore Roosevelt opened the door to the use of executive orders as a lawmaking tool. It should be closed and locked.

Theodore Roosevelt's cousin, Franklin, holds the record for most executive orders. He issued 3,522 and then asked for an enlargement of the executive branch. The Executive Office of the President was started with the Reorganization Act of 1939. It established the foundation of this executive office with its special advisors, or czars as the press calls them today. From its humble beginning, this organization has continued with unchecked growth until more than thirty special advisors are on the payroll today. The actual number of people employed by the office is blurred by assignments-on-loan from other departments, and so forth, but budget estimates top 400 individuals. The people in this office establish national policy and regulations without accountability to the people, other than what the president chooses.

When President Washington established his cabinet he set it up with four appointments. Today, the cabinet is almost as large as the first Senate. This runaway growth started with the Reorganization Plan of 1953 that allowed the president to reorganize executive branch departments as long as neither house of Congress passed a legislative veto. Congress thought is was okay until the Supreme Court declared the legislative veto unconstitutional. With the veto gone, all Congress can do is restrict funds for the purpose, but if the president vetoes their restriction, it is often impossible to override the veto. The power in the provisions of the 1953 plan should be reversed.

Today there are 15 cabinet positions, and 7 more cabinet level positions including the White House Chief of Staff, Director of the Office of Management and Budget, Administrator of the EPA, and others. It takes a big scale to weigh the papers of board laws that are generated by this group of bureaucrats.

EXECUTIVE ORDERS must be supported by a specific clause in the Constitution or by power delegated to the President by Congress. They are published in the Federal Register with the same weight as Congressional law. Until the early 1900s, executive orders were unannounced and undocumented when they were issued. Since this tool was used primarily for instructions to the executive staff it was kept more or less as an internal document. Theodore Roosevelt's extreme application of the executive order changed how they were handled and recorded.

The power of the executive order to become law at the notion of one individual has opened the door to dictatorial temptation. It was an executive order by Franklin Roosevelt that removed Japanese Americans to internment camps during World War Two; this is an injustice that remains an embarrassment to this day. In some cases it became necessary to appeal to the Supreme Court. In 1952 Harry Truman famously used an executive order to place all steel mills under federal control in his response to crippling strikes. Bill Clinton tried to use an executive order in 1995 to prohibit federal contracts with companies that had strikebreakers on their payroll. Presidents mean well in most cases, but the temptation is too great for one individual to place personal beliefs above the beliefs and wishes of the people. Wars have been fought using executive orders, and the wisdom of the Congress in transferring this power may be due for review.

THE EXECUTIVE OFFICE OF THE PRESIDENT has grown beyond limits in a manner similar to the misuse of executive orders. The White House Chief of Staff supervises three levels of officials: Assistant to the President, Deputy Assistant to the President, and Special Assistant to the President. These Special Assistants are more commonly known as the special advisors, or czars. They're called czars because they have become independent lawmakers with no accountability to the people in the way of votes, or confirmation by elected representatives. There are a few positions that are confirmed by the Senate, but these are the exception rather than the rule. The Office of Homeland Security started in this office until it was boosted to a Cabinet position. All of the Homeland Security rules that intrude into individual privacy were made without the approval of American citizens. It was all done in the name of the security of the country, just like it has been strong-armed into law in other countries before.

More than thirty of these little dictators decide and impose public policy upon the American people with little restraint, and without approval of the Congress. The people elect their legislators and the president. The Supreme Court judges and Cabinet members are appointed by the president and confirmed by elected senators. But special advisors are not tied directly or indirectly to the voters by confirmation. These offices are used to establish policy, author legislation, and influence agency rules, and the number of the offices is unlimited and uncontrolled by the Congress. The White House special staff has become a mini-congress working around the elected legislature and using board rule to implement its policies. The limitless increase in its size is a direct indication of the transformation of the federal government toward becoming a centralized democracy.

THE PRESIDENT'S CABINET has matched the growth of executive orders and the White House special staff as the executive branch continues to vacuum power and centralize all decision making under the authority of one person. Not only have the number of cabinet offices grown, as previously discussed, but department rule making is accelerating as well. Each year Americans are overwhelmed by new rules from Agriculture, Commerce, Labor, Health and Human Services, Housing and Urban Development, Education, Transportation, Energy, Veterans Affairs, Homeland Security and others. Even a homeowner who operates an underground lawn sprinkler system must report in to the Environmental Protection Agency. These cabinet agencies seek to control every aspect of daily life.

The danger is that these agencies act through the president making rules that are often in direct opposition to the Congress. The EPA makes its rules for the good of the environment, regardless of the will of Congress and the people. They often cause extreme hardship on innocent citizens in their aggrandized zeal for a higher calling. The EPA was proposed by Richard Nixon and started operations in 1970 by executive order. The House and Senate eventually ratified it. Today, the EPA Administrator is appointed by the President and approved by Congress. Although not a cabinet department, the Administrator serves with cabinet rank.

A group established in the department of the treasury in 1862 by Abraham Lincoln to administer payments on the Civil War debt still exists today. This is the Internal Revenue Service (IRS). With the transition to individual income taxes the IRS department has grown in size to average about 100,000 individuals. It follows the directions of the Congress, but it carries awesome power to establish rules and administer punishment to individual citizens. High-ranking officials have used it to intimidate and harass innocent persons that may disagree with policy. At times, even Congressional members have been bullied into fearful situations.

Richard Nixon started the Occupational Safety and Health Agency in 1970. All government agencies are started with good intentions, but this agency also makes independent rules, standards, and enforcement actions.

Today, the Department of Health and Human Services (HHS) has been a regular newsmaker with its strong-arm rules and bullying tactics. This department was originally named the Department of Health Education and Welfare until 1979 when the Department of Education was spun off on its own by Jimmy Carter. The new Patient Protection and Affordable Care Act has fallen under the jurisdictions of HHS and IRS, so now there are more determinations of rules, waivers, and penalties by these agencies.

NO INDIVIDUAL OR BRANCH of the government can be trusted with the kind of power that has developed in the executive branch. Government is a force like fire. It is a dangerous service to the people that can become a terrible master if allowed to grow outside the boundaries of the Constitution. The powerful growth of the executive branch indicates the strong trend toward a centralized federal government with the people's power wrested from them and left in the hands of a governing class. Americans must decide whether they wish to yield their liberty to the central city, or accept their responsibility for self-government and correct it.

Congress let this happen. A century or more of congressmen have become a part of the governing class, rather than true representatives of the people. They serve with good intentions, but in the slang of Washington-society, they are quickly co-opted. Americans must insist that Congress veto and withdraw the lawmaking authority of the executive branch.

When the federal government oversteps its bounds of authority, the people must appeal to the standard of the Constitution, and Congress must return the power to people. The Congress must implement laws to reverse the overzealous ambition of Theodore

Roosevelt and his successors. Congress must confine executive orders to the executive staff, and its executive lawmaking authority revoked. The Executive Office of the President should be strongly reduced in size. It should be used only to support the president's operations, such as assisting with White House protocol. Special Advisors should be abolished and all lawmaking from this office must be stopped and returned to the Congress. Finally, a cut in the size of the Cabinet is past due. It is likely impractical to eliminate delegated laws in the operation of government so long as Congress continues to create huge programs and new rules that require massive implementation. It has grown too large, though, and the people need congressmen that will check this power and accept their responsibility to keep their programs within the Constitution. The country needs congressmen who will review every bill with their first question being, "Is it constitutional?"

Every president swears to uphold the laws of the country, not to make laws. It is time for the provisions of the Tenth Amendment to be restored. Conversely, if the people of this generation have themselves become so corrupted as to need a centralized government, then the United States will become incapable of any other type.

Career Politicians
A Case for Limits

DURING THE DEBATES when the founders of the country were deciding the details for election of Representatives and Senators, there was a great deal of discussion concerning the length of a term of service and whether there should be limits. A typical term of office in the state governments in those days was a year. Governors, legislators, and so forth were elected to serve one year. Some delegates at the Constitutional Convention suggested similar plans for members of Congress. Eventually it was agreed to set the terms at two years for members of the House and six years for the Senate. Some delegates wanted to limit the number of terms, but finally it was agreed that the decision would be left in the hands of the people. If the constituency wanted career politicians, then they would be free to elect them to as many terms as wanted, and conversely, if the goal was to replenish offices with new ideas, then the voters could make this selection.

After more than two hundred years of experience with this system, it is apparent that there is an inherent weakness with repeatedly electing career politicians to serve in the legislature. The system of using career politicians has evolved into a governing class in Washington that is detached from the voting public. The governing class is a small but distinct segment of American society that has decided that centralized decision-making should be done by government professionals who know what is best for the country; rather than by the electorate.

In addition, career politicians have morphed into the federal employee system creating a conflict of interest that is detrimental to the voters and taxpayers. Against the wishes of the public, representatives who have made a career of public service also decided they should be treated the same as regular federal employees. As a result, they control the purse strings for federal employees, and thus themselves.

In order to maintain a lifetime of elected service, career representatives are firmly tied to party loyalties. These loyalties crush independent thinking and can lead to skirting the Constitution in favor of party agenda. The stranglehold of parties leaves the voting American with few choices on election day.

The system of career politicians is more the result of powerful political bosses and their parties, rather than free choice, and it has damaged the republic and threatens individual freedom. The iron grip of career politicians and their parties has become another facet of the country's transition to centralized government. The stronger and more entrenched this system becomes, the more the decisions are removed to the central city and the more self-government is extinguished.

Nearly half of the members of Congress are millionaires. Many of them earned their fortunes before joining the Congress as physicians, lawyers, and business owners, but others have reaped the benefits of a lucrative career in public service. The system is not fulfilling its potential for self-government, and it is time, past time, to eliminate these treasure hunters from the rolls of public service.

THE CORE QUESTION is whether the United States should continue to empower the governing class to decide what vested rights should be awarded to Americans, or whether it should move to abolish career politicians as elected representatives?

THE HISTORY OF DEBATES by the founders when they were developing the Constitution covered both length of terms and pay. Benjamin Franklin didn't want the Congress to have the power to set its own pay. During his service in Europe he witnessed the abuses that occurred. He knew the salaries of the British were enormous, and he told the other delegates it could happen here, too. Ultimately his advice on this subject went unheeded, and the First Clause of the Sixth Section of the First Article of the US Constitution reads simply, "The Senators and Representatives shall receive a compensation for their services, ..." The reality today is that many career politicians rely on high pay and benefits as federal employees. They share benefits programs with the federal employee system, which in itself represents a substantial conflict of interest. They occupy both sides of the negotiating table, so to speak, when pay raises and benefits packages are reviewed for federal employees. Enhancements in federal benefits will pass indirectly to the members of Congress.

Wise Ben Franklin hit the mark with his prediction, too. The pay and benefits for legislators have grown from a nominal stipend for public service to large salaries and benefits that are far in excess of what is available to the average American.

James Madison recognized the threat of group thinking by a governing class. He thought the pressures of party and politics could skew independent thinking, especially for the new or weaker members who lack confidence in their own ideas and judgment. What a sharp prediction he made of the situation in Washington today as Congressmen and Senators boast of co-opting new members to prevailing ideas. It epitomizes the distrust of modern government.

America has direct experience with long-standing power and its effect on limiting alternative speech and ideas. The purpose of checks and balances established in the Constitution by the founders was to protect the rights of the minority so that all points of view could be heard and considered. Unfortunately, the pursuit of power and privilege by parties and individuals has obstructed these values at times. One of the most significant instances occurred during roughly twenty years around the Presidency of Franklin Roosevelt. The people repeatedly elected Roosevelt as President and Sam Rayburn as Speaker of the House. Roosevelt maneuvered to reorganize government to suit his agenda, and the combination with Rayburn made it very difficult for opposing views to be voiced on the House floor. Congress, and the American people, recognized the problem by limiting the term of the President to two terms. The Congress left the door open, however, for themselves to continue their own long careers in office.

WHEN A GOVERNING CLASS develops, it has a destructive effect on the Republic. A governing class should not be allowed to form and dominate a democratic republic. The transformation is gradual, and it thwarts freedom in at least four ways.

A centralized governing class stifles independent thought. A long dialog develops and is repeated from one individual to another, and from one TV show to another, until it becomes accepted as fact. The idea of vested rights is an example. Politicians have confused the difference between vested and unalienable rights. The ideas that all people have the right to food, clothing, shelter, and health care, for example, are ideas of vested rights; that is, they are implemented by government statute and similarly can be reversed by government statute. In their rhetoric, these vested rights are often lumped together with discussions of unalienable rights and accepted factually as the same. Sometimes the mistake is innocent; sometimes it's deceitful, nevertheless accepted as fact.

The danger of the same individuals remaining in power for long periods of time is their monopoly on influential positions and their ability to steer a one-sided agenda. They seek a single viewpoint without considering the rights and views of others and smother minority speech. It can be between or within parties. The Blue Dog democrats and the Tea Party republicans are often co-opted into compliance with party lines established by career politicians.

The one-sided agenda was prominent during the Roosevelt and Rayburn coalition that has been discussed. Sam Rayburn was dedicated to Roosevelt's governmental programs, and he used the tremendous power of the Speaker to direct the legislative agenda and decide who was recognized to speak. It was extremely difficult for opposing views to be heard. This became an extreme problem when the power was locked in for a decade or more.

In their zeal to maintain their power hold, the Congress has endorsed a steady transition to bureaucratic rule. The unending growth of rulemaking by executive orders, special advisors in the Executive Office of the President, and cabinet agencies strengthens central power and skirts the authority of the Constitution. Career politicians are separated from the people; they are so entrenched in office they come to believe they better understand what is right for the country.

The governing class has convinced a large part of the American population that candidates for public service must have extensive experience to be competent and effective to run the government. Their long history of constitutional abuses suggests otherwise. The founding fathers believed there would always be a ready supply of honest and reasonable people to occupy government positions. The Constitution is a plain and simple document by design; the intent was that any citizen should be able to read and comprehend it. Unfortunately, the growth and power of political parties make it nearly impossible for an average, un-co-opted individual to seek and win a seat in the Congress.

Members of Congress are sent by the people to consult with one another and to manage the nation's business, not to seek an agenda or blindly support a party line. Instead, they posture and block one another until each session of Congress is stifled. A periodic fresh supply of dedicated representatives would reduce the possibility of a power hold on the Congress and increase the interest in supporting a Constitution based upon public opinion.

LEGISLATORS HAVE BECOME FEDERAL EMPLOYEES, not representatives of the people. They return home to stump for reelection, but truly are citizens of the central city and culture of the governing class. The shift to working for the federal government instead of the people began around 1942 when Congress attempted to add its members to federal benefits plans. Wartime Americans resisted, but in 1946 the persistent Congress won its campaign to become federal employees. For the first 150 years or so, members of Congress did not receive the benefits they receive today. About the only difference today between a federal civil servant and a member of Congress is the requirement to win an election, and this situation blurs their duty to voters.

Not only does a long career on the federal rolls contribute to a conflict of interest in properly managing the federal payroll, but it also contributes to the abuse of the earmark spending privilege, and to extended careers beyond viability. All of these problems develop as each individual seeks increased retirement benefits, life and health insurance, and a federal job if they are defeated in election. Each improvement in federal benefits for regular employees will eventually extend to the Congress. Each earmark bill passed to benefit a special group will cement their grip in the next election. Each year of service they add helps shut out the opposition and adds to their retirement package, until many of them become dotards that are propped up by party comrades for roll call.

THE CONSTITUTION SUFFERS from the ambitions of career politicians, despite their oath to uphold the Constitution. It is their primary job, yet many Congressmen and Senators report for duty without a strong grasp of the Constitution. The simple legacy of the Constitutional Convention is plain and short. The main body of the Constitution has seven articles and there have been twenty-seven amendments attached to it. Instructions for the Congress are specified in the First Article, and the explicit powers of Congress are listed in Section Eight of Article One. It's clear and concise, but many Representatives and Senators appear to prefer to work without reference to it.

Without frequently consulting the law of the Constitution as it is written, the nation is exposed to a Congress that twists the meaning of the national contract by both mistake and intent. Often it has been bent to suit party aims for a social agenda, such as social insurance and health care. In their dual role as both elected representatives and federal employees, the Congress disregards perversions of the Constitution, such as its failure to provide a responsible national budget and cause it to be effective.

The first question from any Congressman or Senator on proposed legislation should be, "Is it constitutional?" Each office should employ their staff to research it and compare the staff report with their individual assessment. When it's determined to have the least doubt, questions should be asked, because the only security of the people of the country lies in the Constitution. If a proposed program does not fall within the framework of the Constitution, but there is evidence that the people may support it, then let the Congress ask the people for a change, an amendment; but, no matter how strong the sentiment of public opinion, the activity of the Congress must never deviate from the provisions of the Constitution until it has been amended. It's basic contract law. If an act isn't contained within the written boundaries of the Constitution, it isn't legal. Ratified changes to the Constitution would stop the constitutionality arguments of social programs such as welfare, food stamps, Social Security, and Medicare.

FIRST STEPS TO PURGE the Congress of professional politicians begin by reversing their membership in federal employee benefits programs and imposing term limits. In order to remove the temptation of a life in Congress, the incentives of high pay and lucrative retirement and health plans should be removed. Pay for members of Congress should never exceed the national average wage for Americans, that is, they shall receive a nominal stipend to partially offset their expenses of service. The combination of low pay without benefits will attract individuals who truly want to serve. Such changes should be effective only from the time a new law is enacted; that is, promises must be kept to those who served under preceding rules.

Concurrent with this change the nation should consider imposing term limits on Congressmen and Senators. It would be the completion of measures that were never finished after term limits were set on the Presidency. If the office of president can be effective over an eight-year period, then it is just as likely that similar limits on Congressmen and Senators will have a good effect, too. Some of the most effective private business executives believe that periodic changes of leadership keep their organizations fresh and vibrant; many think fifteen years should be a maximum limit for a business chief.

There will be much argument against slashing pay and benefits and limiting length of service. A typical preparation today for public office includes a law degree. There will be strong argument that to get the best and most capable people will require competitive pay and political credentials. The forefathers couldn't have disagreed more. Benjamin Franklin said there always will be a supply of good men who were willing to serve, and he believed the less the pay the greater the honor. The argument against high pay requirements can be found in the abundant supply of firefighters, police officers, and military personnel that serve for love of country rather than love of power and profit.

In addition to token salaries and term limits, new laws are needed to abolish gifts to federal officials and to require recurrent constitutional training. All Congressional expenses should be limited to government business at conservative per diem rates. These people are representatives, not royalty, and it is time they are returned to strict operational expenses. Gifts to members of Congress should be eliminated altogether. It's inappropriate. They are at the service of the people, and gifts from lobbyists or others are truly the property of the people. Worry over gift amounts and their circumstances are pure foolishness that is best corrected by completely eliminating the activity.

In order to emphasize allegiance to and understanding of the Constitution, each member of Congress should be required to complete recurrent training on the provisions of the Constitution before being allowed to be seated in the respective chamber. The Constitution is easy to read, short, direct, and clear by design. Each individual takes an oath to uphold it, so it is not unreasonable of the people to ask that all public servants be well versed in its provisions.

Many of the proposed changes can be implemented by simple legislation. Of course, term limits will require the ultimate change, a constitutional amendment. It is likely unreasonable to expect career legislators to initiate an amendment that will ultimately turn them out of office. In this situation, the people must turn to the provisions of Article Five of the Constitution that permits the application of two-thirds of the States to call a convention for proposing an amendment, and to make it law when ratified by three-fourths of the States. It's the wonderful safety valve left to the people by the forefathers.

It's time for a change. It's time to elect good people who are willing to serve at great sacrifice for a limited period of time in order to serve the people that elected them and to advance the idea of self-government through public opinion. It could be the virtual end of the governing class in America and the restoration of the great republican government.

The Supreme Court
A Case for Revision

MOST AMERICANS today accept the absolute power of the Supreme Court to decide matters of constitutionality. Remarkably, many of the early constitutional minds did not accept the Court's absolute power. In fact, the idea of self-government is built upon the concept that only the people have the power to make law, and a lot of the founders believed the only role of the Supreme Court should be to insure the people's law is followed. In sympathy with keeping the Court confined to deciding cases based on the Constitution, there were alternative thoughts by some of the founders that there should be constitutional provisions to overrule Court decisions when it was determined that the Court had stepped outside its constitutional authority.

When the country's founders developed the idea of the national Supreme Court they believed a guardian of the Constitution was needed. The Constitution would be the supreme law of the people, and in order to protect it against violations by the Congress, by the President, and by the States, the constitutional architects established a Supreme Court to keep these branches of government within their assigned authorities. Their idea, of course, was that only the people could establish the laws through their representatives and the common law jury process. The Supreme Court, then, would be assigned the responsibility for insuring the laws complied with the Constitution.

During debates when the Constitution was formed there was discussion on how much power should be conferred to the Court. Some delegates were proponents of lifetime appointments for judges while others thought a fixed term of office would be more appropriate. A second argument developed over recourse on Court decisions. One group believed the decisions of the Court should be final and binding, while other delegates thought veto power should be retained by the Congress to protect the people.

Ultimately the weakness of human nature has resulted in instances of substitution of political agenda for law. There has been maneuvering by both presidents and congresses to influence the

Court, not only its rulings, but also the composition of its members. Falling victim to these pressures, the men and women of the Court have invented new arguments around the Constitution to conform to political policy, and they have allowed the Court to become interested in public policy more than law. Thomas Jefferson was afraid that the Supreme Court would begin interpreting the Constitution by squeezing its text to invent new arguments around it to conform to political policy. His fear of individual weakness has materialized.

THE CORE QUESTION is whether Supreme Court Justices should be appointed for life and without checks and balances on their decisions?

THE HISTORY OF THE COURT'S DEVELOPMENT begins with the earliest debate over its authority and the terms for justices. The delegates to the Constitutional Convention had experienced the subservience of English judges to the King, and they wanted to prevent similar relationships from developing in the United States. The monarch or other authoritative methods could be used to remove English judges if their decisions were met with displeasure. It corrupted the judges and left the people unprotected by juries. The founders at home planned a system based on common law protections. Two questions for implementing their system were how to protect the judges from corruptive influence, and how to protect the people from corrupt judges

The Constitution's creators did not lightly consider the appointment of justices to office for life. Although neither man was present at the convention, both John Adams and Thomas Jefferson offered written opinions on the two alternatives that were considered for administration of a Supreme Court. John Adams, for example, believed justices should be individuals that were very experienced in the law and who had exemplary morals. He feared the corruption of justices if they were subject to removal from office at the whim of the Executive or Legislature, such as in England. As a result, he believed justices should be subservient to no one and appointed for life. The idea still makes sense, and this is the system inherited from the founders that remains in existence today.

Jefferson, on the other hand, did not think the Supreme Court should be set up to rule without checks and balances, and that no human could be trusted for life. He thought it to be dangerous doctrine to consider judges as the ultimate arbiters of all constitutional questions. It was his fear that it could leave the country vulnerable to the authority of a small group of individuals. Jefferson agreed that a judiciary independent of a king or executive alone is a good thing, but he also believed it was a mistake to leave it independent of the will of the nation, at least a republican nation. After the Constitution was completed, he wrote that he thought it was an error to omit the caution of making a judge removable on the address of both houses.

The final solution is written in the Constitution, substantially in Articles Three and Six. The First Section of Article Three authorizes the organization of the Supreme Court and that justices, "shall hold their offices during good behavior." Article Six establishes the Constitution as the supreme law of the land and binds all federal and state officers to the Constitution by oath.

Once the new government was established, the long process of developing theories of constitutional law began almost immediately. Two theories of the Court's adjudicating role have been described as judicial review and judicial interpretation. Judicial review would be the doctrine that legislative and executive actions are subject to review, and judicial interpretation would be the mode of judicial thought that may be applied to interpret the Constitution.

Maneuvering by career politicians to slant Court opinions in their favor slowly developed until it has become somewhat prevalent in US government today. Presidents attempt to organize the Court, using their appointments, until the Court seems to be divided on most opinions according to the political inclination of individual justices. When there is a vacancy on the Supreme Court today, the political maneuvering that occurs to slant the Court in an intended direction perfectly illustrates the political nature of the Court. Instead of a jury of impartial judges to rule on the content of the Constitution, it has evolved into a political group with the same passions for party, power, and privilege as those joined in the quest for power and distinction in the other branches of government. When Franklin Roosevelt began the move toward supreme federal power with his ambitious programs for involvement in private lives, he tried to use the Court to support his agenda. When this failed, he tried to increase the size of the Court from nine justices to fifteen so he could appoint six more justices during his administration that would support his New Deal plans and slant the Court in his favor. Fortunately, this ambitious grab for dictatorial power was rejected by the Legislature.

The political nature of some Courts is evident when they have announced that their decisions were based upon public policy and modern doctrine. The danger of this idea lies in the opportunity for a small group of justices to assume the power of the people to decide public opinion. It defeats the entire precept of a self-ruling people.

JUDICIAL THEORY of the Constitution often begins with the comparison of common law and parliamentary sovereignty. The US Constitution is based upon common and civil law. Common-law judges are seen as sources of law, and are capable of creating or retracting legal rules. Conversely, in civil law applications the judges apply the law with no power to create or eliminate legal rules. When disputes arise in the US under the common law basis, then the Supreme Court could become the arbiter. Where parliamentary sovereignty is the law, then the statutes of the legislature are absolute and cannot be set aside under this doctrine. Rules of parliamentary sovereignty are used in various forms by European countries, and in some cases their constitution expressly forbids court ruling on questions of constitutionality of primary legislation. In this case, the power of the legislative branch is somewhat unchecked by the court.

Instead, the US Constitution establishes the Supreme Court with the power to overturn both laws established by the legislature and board laws created by agencies of the executive branch. Two methods for the approach the Court takes when deciding a case have been described as judicial review and judicial interpretation. Judicial review identifies the power of the Court to examine legislative and executive actions and their possible invalidation; it has become a key check on the other two branches. Thomas Jefferson, however, worried about the total power to invalidate laws, because he thought it allowed the judiciary to assume the authorities of the other branches.

The second mode of thought is usually called judicial interpretation. This refers to Court activity as it reviews the constitutional documents and legislation to determine meaning and applicability to a given case. The authors of the Constitution attempted to use plain language for the clear understanding of all citizens, but cultural changes and unforeseen developments through the centuries have left the Court with some difficulty in applying the original meaning to cases today. New legislation may include confusion for a variety of reasons. Current examples include the massive health care bill that was put together and hastily passed without adequate time for legislators to review it contents. The magnitude of the Court's assignment to review the meaning of thousands of pages in the bill is unimaginable, and it is practically guaranteed that nine individuals will not read such an enormous amount of legislation in the same way. When new legislation is enacted this way it is more likely to step on the Constitution.

The difficulty of applying the Constitution to large numbers of massive bills has become overwhelming, and the opportunity for diverting from the will of the people is magnified. Sometimes words have straightforward meaning, but more often today, there is doubt in their meaning that must be resolved by the Court. In practice, the Court's interpretation can result in broad changes to the law.

Without question the Constitution confers extraordinary responsibility and power on justices to determine their ruling. It must be extremely difficult to decide, and neither method, that is review or interpretation, is a perfect solution. The will of the people is the ultimate law in America, and it should not be decided by nine individuals attempting to carry out an awesome responsibility using rudimentary methods. As sure as new technologies and evolving cultures complicate the application of law, so has this same evolution developed a need for changes in the checks and balances of today's government.

As a result of the difficult, and somewhat limited, methods used to decide constitutional law, it is natural that the humanity of the Court often results in decisions that are less than objective. The temptation to insert personal beliefs into decisions is often called judicial activism, and the resistance to it is termed judicial restraint. Today, the Supreme Court appears as divided as ever on lines of personal beliefs. Remarkably, the positions taken by justices frequently line up with the political views of the party of the president in power that appointed them. They are often called conservative or liberal in their decisions in the same vein as political parties.

Justices have responded to activist accusations that an activist court is a court that makes decisions that aren't liked. Of course, the idea of judicial restraint that encourages judges to limit the exercise of their own power could not exist and would not be necessary without the reality of judicial activism.

The true situation is that justices are imperfect and subject to the same human frailties as ordinary citizens. The application of judicial review and interpretation is a necessity that cannot be eliminated, because no law can be perfectly written, no matter how loyal to the Constitution the writer may intend. The danger that persists from this situation, though, is that the political struggle to establish a Court with unbalanced views can certainly result in a Court that wields its decisions against the true will of the law of the people. The will of the people's law is the Court's true calling and reason for existence.

Judicial administration has been the natural transition from judicial oversight to a mixture with political influences. Because there is not provision in the Constitution for checks and balances on the Court's decision, the opportunity for activism is strong and results with distortion of the Constitution. The Court's history includes confessions that it has been compelled in some decisions to meet social needs or to comply with established public policy. Few could agree that the intended purpose of the Court is to carry out social needs or public policy. It opens the country to abuses. For example, slavery was once the public policy of the country. These are not issues to be decided by the few.

The shift to a political court expressing influenced ideals is a direct result of maneuvering by the President and Senate to stack the Court to support majority agenda. Now the Court has become split between conservative and liberal dogma until it is ruled by its activism instead of its loyalty to the Constitution. By allowing its personal views and interpretations to creep into its decisions, its activism has allowed judicial administration of state schools, prisons, and employment practices. No amount of constructive constitutional interpretation could justify a small, privileged group of lawyers to enter into people's lives and make decisions for them.

LIFE APPOINTMENTS to justice positions add to the imbalance of constitutional power and open the door for independent abuses. The history of the Court's development explains the logic of the majority of the Constitutional Convention's delegates to allow court justices to be objective in their duty without pressure or prejudice. Unfortunately, it hasn't worked out that way, and the opposing views are compelling, too. Jefferson knew human nature; he knew man is not made to be trusted for life, especially if secured against all liability to account for his actions. He thought life appointments would make the justices independent of the nation. An alternative system is needed to insure justices are under no undue pressure, but they should not be free for a life of political influence.

CHANGE IS NEEDED to reverse the independence of the Supreme Court from the law of the people. A governing system based upon the rule of the people through public opinion and the provisions of common law must not be subjected to the rule of nine individuals. The appropriate changes are fixed terms and limits for justices, veto power by the people's representatives, and firm qualification requirements for justice positions.

Appointment terms and limits are needed to reduce the Court's independence from the law of the people. Jefferson suggested Supreme Court terms ranging from four to six years, and then renewable by the President and Senate. Building upon Jefferson's views, it is suggested that appointment of justices should be for a fixed term, not to exceed six years. If the President and Senate approve the conduct of a justice at the end of a first term, then a second appointment for a fixed term may be made, but no judge may serve more than two terms at the bench of the Supreme Court.

In order to protect the lawmaking authority of American citizens, a veto power over Supreme Court decisions should be authorized. Here again, Jefferson boldly offered his idea for veto power such that the vote of two-thirds of the Congress or three-fourths of the State Legislatures could overturn a Court decision. This provision provides a safeguard of the law of the people founded on the idea of common law. Although not as strong as parliamentary sovereignty, it returns the ultimate power to the people without a total surrender to the group of nine.

Finally, qualifications for justices should be identified, such as is done in the Constitution for Congressmen, Senators, and the President. Perhaps qualifications should include experience requirements. When justices must consider the laws of the people, bench experience working in real situations with the people is far more valuable than a background limited to academic experience in isolation from the people. By identifying specific criteria, candidates could be screened against minimal standards before being submitted by the President for approval by the Senate. The idea would be to reduce the political posturing that so often retards the approval process of justices. If a candidate meets minimal criteria, there is little else a Senate should do to block an appointment if a record of good behavior is in evidence.

The history of the Court and the political environment around it today are reason enough to consider the changes outlined. Obviously, a constitutional amendment is required, but once understood by common Americans, it is likely that they would not only support, but also insist upon, term limits and veto power. Americans are disillusioned with the Court's inconsistencies, reversals, and disregard for the authority of a self-governing people. The Court is seated at the pleasure of the people, and it is time to return the power to them.

Can Government Make Jobs?
A Case for Reality

US ECONOMIC LEADERSHIP appears to be vanishing. It may be gone, already. Perhaps nothing perplexes and worries the mature American public more, especially those who experienced the grand era of US inventiveness and economic leadership in the last century. Normally accustomed to a strong bounce after a steep fall, the recovery from the 2008 economic decline has been a slow one. Unemployment remains high and economic growth is at a comparative snail's pace. It has a lot of Americans wondering what has happened to the US economy.

Complex market forces, such as supply and demand, are primarily influenced by the activity and health of three parts: individuals, corporations, and the government. Both the government and private individuals are hampered by burdensome debt. Healthy corporations may not carry huge debt, but are reluctant to invest until their confidence is restored in the demand side of market forces.

The break of 2008 was the result of government manipulation of the housing market and the unrestrained greed of financial opportunists. The extraordinary boom that preceded the decline obscured the weakness of the whole economy. This weakness slowly progressed for thirty years or so, as a result of growing debt and the steady migration of jobs to foreign sources. The difference in the standard of living between the US and other countries is so large that it is impossible for American labor to compete with the lower labor rates offshore; at least, no one so far has figured out a way to offset the differential. First, manufacturing labor was affected, but today the pressure has expanded to service call centers, accounting, engineering, and marketing functions. The combined economic pressure of high debt and unemployment has reduced market demand, and it is likely to continue for several years. The American juggernaut may be lost for a generation.

Government has tried to fill the void in response. It has printed money, dropped interest rates, borrowed deeper to support public assistance programs, and generated phantom jobs using subsidies and credits. Unemployment benefits and welfare roles are bursting at the seams as the federal safety net is extended to extraordinary limits. The ratio of productive workers to idled citizens has tipped until there are not enough employed citizens to support the unemployed. In response, the US continues to borrow money, primarily from foreign sources, to plug the hole. Now the debt has increased beyond the ability of the national work force to carry it. Eventually the central government will be forced to raise taxation to repay the costs of its artificial world, and this will drag down industry and impede American competitive opportunities.

In its first two hundred years Americans were producers. The country was busy at work in agriculture, mining, and manufacturing activities that expanded the real wealth of the country and raised the standard of living. In the twenty-first century, though, the country has become a nation of consumers, not producers. Jobs in America largely do not add to its wealth, but merely consume the wealth created in other places. Banking, marketing, entertainment, sociology, education, health care, and similar jobs are all needed in American society, but these workers consume the real wealth created by others. Without strong new sources of real wealth, accompanied by prudent financial management, the economy stagnates and the debt grows disproportionately.

The government promises Americans to fix it by making jobs through its use of regulations and federal hiring. More federal workers mean more jobs, it says. Tax credits, subsidies, and other financial gimmicks are offered to stimulate hiring. The inescapable fact, though, is that it is impossible for any government to create a job, because government itself is a cost to the working citizens of the country. Adding a federal job merely increases the cost of government, and does not add to the wealth of the country. Taxes, or worse, more borrowing must cover the cost of these jobs. When an employer is lured into adding a job in order to claim a tax credit, it is often a phantom job that will vanish as soon as the credit is exhausted. Subsidies to improve the market have a similar effect; that is, they cause artificially low prices that are only possible through taxes paid by working Americans. The housing and mortgage markets are great examples.

The American economy is strangled by government intervention. It has not been allowed to ebb and flow according to natural market forces. American innovation and creativity has been transferred to other countries with the jobs that accompany it. The US productive work force is left languishing and waiting. The national spirit is broken.

THE CORE QUESTION is whether the US government can help the economy? Is it possible for federal intervention to create jobs?

JOB MIGRATION AND GROWING DEBT have troubled the US economy for decades. Early labor pressures on American companies began in the late seventies and early eighties. Each year companies were faced with competition from other companies that were using primarily Mexican labor to produce their products at lower cost. Their labor rates were barely a dollar an hour, and average US workers earned seven to fifteen dollars an hour for similar work. Many companies turned to automation in an attempt to reduce the labor content in their product. This worked for a time in some applications, but soon American companies began building new factories in Mexico and other countries, and set up machinery and equipment with US technology. Eventually, the rush to Mexico and places south became an avalanche, and companies began closing plants and laying off US workers. Those laid off were told they would need to retrain themselves for jobs requiring greater technological skill.

The changes in China followed and opened the door to stronger pressures on both US and Mexican labor. Many Asian operations paid about a dollar a day to their workers. This was less than an eighth of the wages of new prosperity in Mexico. It didn't take long for US companies to continue the transfer to Asian companies, and to build Asian factories. The arithmetic was somewhat simple. If the product had high labor content, sold a large number of units each year, and was small enough to ship at low enough cost, then it was a candidate for Asian production.

Today, the US is left with shells of deserted factories everywhere. US cities that had been prosperous during the manufacturing boom of the twentieth century resemble ghost towns after a gold rush. The workers left behind were told not to worry. Their jobs would be replaced by new, high-pay, technical jobs. Only the more mundane, low-skill jobs would be shipped offshore. In the meantime, they would have to retrain for the jobs requiring the higher technological skill. It really didn't work out that way, though, because the US companies began transferring their technologies and training foreign workers, too, so high-skill and advanced-knowledge jobs are migrating, too.

As companies became more successful in setting up factories and developing foreign relationships, job transfers included office jobs. Customer service centers, and marketing research activities were moved to Singapore, the Philippines, and other popular labor supply markets. Spurred by the phenomenal power of computers and the Internet, it soon became popular to set up engineering technical centers and accounting activities in India, China, and elsewhere. Financial managers discovered the cost of one American engineer could be used to hire three Indian engineers with PhD educations. Many American engineers and technicians spent their last working days training a foreign counterpart to use the technology they spent years developing themselves. Once the technology transfer was complete, they were discharged.

The transfer of jobs out of the US is fully developed and is a large contributor to the stubborn unemployment numbers that have persisted since the economic decline of 2008. These jobs likely will not return in the near future. It will require some adjustment of economic equilibrium to restore American competitiveness. Those caught in transition must seek new sources of income, if they haven't given up.

In the meantime, US debt continues to grow. The amount of private individual debt continued its steady increase until it burst and collapsed around 2007. This restricts the ability of consumers to spur economic growth.

Government debt has grown unrestrained throughout its history. It is the direct result of poor management of the nation's business by Washington. Combined with long and expensive wars, the development of social spending on welfare and social insurance programs have built a debt obligation that may be insurmountable. The debt problem persists at all levels including federal, state, and local governments. Although the national debt has grown steadily since the country was born, its growth in the last thirty years has been enormous. The federal government routinely overspends its intake from tax and revenue sources by more than $1 trillion each year. This overspending habit has contributed to the extraordinary growth of the national debt. Total debt in 1955 was about $289 billion, and it has generally doubled every ten years until reaching about $16 trillion in 2013. At this rate it will likely grow to $19 trillion or higher by 2015. This inordinate debt is a drag on the US economy, similar to a private company that has built huge debt and struggles to dig out of it.

Simply stated, American jobs are gone, never to return until the country can again be competitive. There are innovators who hope there may be help from new and more economical machines to help bring jobs home. For their parts, federal and state governments must cut their debt, pare their government, and reduce their tax burdens in order to bring back real job producers. If they don't, then probably there will not be a significant shift in the jobs market, and American society will continue its transformation into a nation of consumers on the dole.

ELEMENTARY ECONOMIC PRINCIPLES explain the different types of jobs and how they are developed. It starts with the ideas of real wealth and jobs that add value to a society. Real wealth is the development of tangible resources. In general, there are three forms of real wealth from agriculture, mining, and manufacturing. The labor to develop these activities adds hard, physical wealth to society. For much of American history its strength was built around its phenomenal breadbasket, its bountiful natural resources, and its unparalleled manufacturing technology. In contrast with real wealth, trading and financial methods can be used to build intangible wealth. Interest on savings, for example, is a form of paper wealth. Similarly, rising stock prices show up nicely in individual accounts, but it is all on paper and can go up in smoke overnight.

Two types of jobs are usually recognized and are often called value-added and non-value-added jobs. The difference is described in the character of the work done. In manufacturing, for example, the machinist that constructs a product is considered to have a value-added job, because the work accomplished converts a raw piece of material into a product for use by consumers. The real wealth of the country is increased. Conversely, a fork truck driver that delivers the raw material to the machinist accomplishes a non-value-added job; that is, delivery activity is simply moving the material. The fork driver's job is essential for efficient operation and higher output, but it is not the direct labor that actually converts the raw material into a product. The same material-handling comparison can be made for all real wealth operations. In agriculture, the person who picks the fruit adds value while the person who hauls it away does not; similarly, a coalmine operation has its parallel.

Building upon the concepts of real wealth and value-added work it is possible to draw a similarity between real jobs and public support jobs. Real jobs are the result of providing a product or service at a strong value that leads to more sales and more revenue and require more individuals to keep up with demand. This includes all value-added and non-value-added jobs that both produce real wealth and that increase demand for products. Public support jobs, though, are a community cost that must be carried by those engaged with real jobs. Although many public support jobs are necessary for an orderly and happy society, such as police and firefighters, they are economically defined strictly as non-value-added work that are a support cost. This same non-value-added classification applies to virtually every federal, state, and local job. Government support jobs consume part of the wealth created by real jobs.

How to create real jobs has become the central debate since the prolonged economic decline of 2008. In general, there are two ideas on how jobs are developed. There are the supply and demand theorists who believe jobs are created by market demands. Other economists believe technology and financial innovation will lead to new jobs. According to the supply and demand concept, supply and demand will seek a balance. These interactions are affected by heavy, burdensome debt and massive job migration, which cause falling market demand. Job creation stalls or dies altogether.

Alternatively, some theorists believe the main constraint on job growth is supply, and that technical and financial innovation will improve productivity and foster growth of the labor force. This has been true somewhat for much of the country's history. Henry Ford's assembly line ideas are an example of this principle that has advanced beyond imagination. In addition, the concept of relying on technical innovation really doesn't consider the second side of the market idea of demand. If there is no demand, there is no need for more supply, and the market dies. Foreign producers meet demand today, and healthy corporations are criticized for "sitting on mountains of cash." Of course they are. With diminished market demand, smart business managers won't hire people to stand around, nor will they buy more equipment to stand idle. Corporate investment will naturally resume when signaled by natural market forces.

Financial innovation has been used in the effort to create jobs. The government has been the principal leader to add tax credits, print more money, implement subsidies, and raise taxes. The idea of financial innovation to develop the economy has turned out to be misleading and more damaging than helpful. The current extended time period with monetary interest rates essentially at zero has substantially reduced the power of the Federal Reserve to manipulate the economy. Fortunes have been made, but not by hardworking, productive workers, but by slick bankers and speculators. The money created isn't real wealth, but fantasy money. Through its incremental increases in the money supply, often called quantitative easing, stock and security values have apparent increases, but the true value largely has not changed. Savings accounts may be about the same as before the crash, but the true spending value hasn't really increased. The values of these accounts can be wiped out in a day, according to the whims of traders.

Other financial innovations include credits and subsidies, but savvy companies won't hire more people just because government offers to pay part of new salaries. There must be a market demand to justify adding more people and cost to their budget structure. The jobs that have been lost to foreign sources are gone, never to return unless or until the situation is equalized. The only alternative is to develop new industry and new markets that need more people. The difference today is that new jobs are sent offshore as fast as they are developed.

GOVERNMENT CONTROLS have become the perceived safety net by many citizens. For the believers in government controls with its theoretical specialists, it is natural to turn to the government to fix the economy. They expect government actions to create jobs through more programs and financial manipulation of market forces. The truth is that the government can't make real jobs. Raising taxes or printing more money in order to put more people on a government payroll will never solve the productivity problem the country faces. This only adds to the debt, which is one of the main problems in the first place. When the nation reduced its production of real wealth, the ability of the working person to earn and grow was restricted or lost altogether.

It should never be forgotten that government employment does not add productive jobs; they are a cost to the country. Unlike jobs that produce real wealth, government workers don't produce a thing for the country, but a certain number of them are needed and should be recognized as a necessary cost of running the country. Adding more bureaucrats, teachers, police officers, or other public service workers does not add jobs; it adds cost for the taxpayers. Just like a private company must keep these support costs reasonable and in check, so should the federal government keep its costs low, instead of selling public service jobs to Americans as jobs that have been created.

Many of government's actions to create jobs are directed toward the government sector itself. Although some government jobs may contribute to maintaining infrastructure, such as road repair, in reality the move is simply inflating the government cost structure, or budget, that has been established for this purpose. Instead of streamlining the government, it is adding bulk to the operation. As a matter of fact, many government jobs added in this manner will never be reduced, and the government just continues to grow and consume the nation's wealth. Subsidies and regulations add to the size of government, too. Every new program and every new subsidy requires more regulators on the payroll at taxpayer expense. These aren't new jobs, these don't add productivity, but instead, they build a bloated cost structure that America can't afford.

The reality is that government can never create jobs that will contribute to the nation's health, productivity, or growth. Adam Smith, the brilliant Scottish philosopher who is considered the father of modern economics, explained that the number of workers that can be kept employed must be in proportion to resources, such as capital and income. It means employment in the country can never realistically exceed its production. No regulation or government manipulation of commerce can increase the job demand beyond what the capital and production of society can maintain. In short, jobs are created or lost as a result of supply and demand in the marketplace, which is related to the real wealth created by the country. Government can't create this, and only does harm when it tries.

When America stops producing, it stops producing jobs.

Financial innovation and government intervention create a bubble of phantasmal make-work jobs at great cost to those who are creating real wealth. When the bubble collapses, so does the country.

THE CONCLUSION is that jobs will not return until US labor is competitive again, and that the best help the government can offer is to streamline government operations to reduce national costs that will unleash the phenomenal innovative American spirit. Following the example of a private company that finds its cost structure too bloated, its debt too large, and must cut its costs to the bone to remain competitive, American government operations should be pared for maximum efficiency in order to relieve the cost burdens of its taxes and to implement cost competitive business taxes.

The real government solution is to eliminate the debt and establish a competitive tax system that allows Americans to compete again in the world. These actions are likely to restore lost jobs from foreign countries to American soil and stimulate market growth. Market growth means market demand and real, productive jobs that contribute to the real wealth of the USA.

Cutting the debt will mean cutting the size of the government and eliminating many of its programs. When a department goes, so goes the spending on its programs. Subsidies and tax credits would become a footnote for historians. The cutbacks will allow true tax cuts that can help companies challenge both national and global competitors. No matter how disguised, government subsidies and job creation programs only add cost and size to government operations and continue to cripple the efforts of private citizens to compete in the world market, to grow, and to prosper. American achievement is not the result of government planning, but it is the result of the American freedom to compete and grow despite government programs.

The innovative American spirit persists in searching for answers. Robotics inventors believe the costs of machinery may soon be reduced enough to economically offset the labor differential between American and foreign labor. But as long as the governing class, with its theoretical scholastic ideas, continues to restrain Americans, tax Americans, regulate Americans, and add Americans to the dole, the country will continue to languish for years to come. It is conceivable that America's strength may be lost to a new era of following the rest of the world.

Government must free the American spirit for innovation and achievement. The US government should stop its interference in the free market system and let its citizens live in freedom. This will be the only solution to lost jobs and a flagging economy. If the income tax system were eliminated, or at least the government drain on corporate earnings reduced, it is likely that the US economy would return to a booming economy. Given half a chance to compete, the ingenuity and productivity of a freed people will release a pent up economy and initiate one of the greatest booms of prosperity the country has ever seen.

Government Unions
A Case for Exclusion

ALL INDIVIDUALS HAVE THE RIGHT to join together in the common cause of bargaining with their employer if there is a majority of workers in favor of it. It is as important to American freedom as the Bill of Rights, and it should be fiercely protected. Union membership can offer a sense of security to its members as they seek a common cause for fair treatment by their employers.

Conversely, every grant of security to one group of individuals results with insecurity for another. This occurs in a union environment when non-members are excluded from the free opportunity to compete for the same jobs. Many states now have laws against this situation in an effort to balance the opportunities for all citizens.

Organized labor in government jobs, however, is a special situation that can result with severe conflicts of interest and unfair practices. In many cases government unions breach the rights of taxpaying citizens. This results in situations where union dues are used to support the very government officials that negotiate the union contract. It is virtually impossible for elected officials to objectively discuss the provisions of a contract with the people who were instrumental in securing their election.

THE CORE QUESTION is whether collective bargaining with organized labor unions should be prohibited for government workers?

THE ORIGINAL AIM OF UNIONS in America was security and protection. It was an admirable goal to obtain reasonable hours, a safer working environment, and a fair wage for their efforts. During the era of union development it was common for employers to be selfish, cruel, disrespectful, and greedy. They set long hours and demanded overtime attendance at a whim. Little attention was given to comfort or safety of workers, and even though needed, the chances of spending money to improve it were slim. Perhaps the worst injury occurred when there were too many desperate candidates for the same job, and ruthless managers gave in to their greed to reduce wages. The employed worker could either take the pay cut or exchange places with the hopeless unemployed.

After many bloody and deadly battles, unions won a place in free commerce with the help of the federal government. Conditions improved. Unfortunately, union leadership was equally susceptible to the weakness of the flesh. As their power grew, they became no less demanding, no less selfish and cruel, and no less greedy than the hard-hearted managers they dealt with. Without adequate controls the operations of many union organizations suffered the turmoil of corruption and dishonesty.

The union movement continued to grow for decades, and union leaders quickly realized the importance of growth for their survival. They worked to enter every facet of business and industry. A larger membership meant a growing union career, power, and privilege. Eventually, the unions found a huge opportunity with government workers. Government workers, who were supposed to be public servants, such as fire fighters, police officers, and teachers, began to demand more pay and benefits. With their new found power, and a healthy dose of greed, these same workers were willing to hold the taxpayer hostage in order to obtain their goals. Their quest for security resulted with insecurity for the public.

Even when the terms are amicable between taxpayers and union workers, there is an element of inefficiency and extra expense that the taxpayers must bear. Taxpayers must pay the cost of union dues, negotiations, and union management. A union is an extra cost for any operation. Without it, the cost of a business, or government operation, will be less. It is an extra cost demanded by the workers in order to insure their security. Dues, for instance, may be withheld from wages, but the wages are artificially inflated to cover the cost of the dues; the business, or taxpayer, must cover this difference.

One of the largest inequities between government union workers and the average taxpayer is the difference in retirement benefits. This difference is not entirely new. The acceptance of modest pay with generous retirement benefits for government workers has been long established. Gradually, though, the pay rates have increased until the average government employee earns more than a comparable average taxpayer, and the retirement benefits have grown out of proportion, too. Many government workers are able to retire when they reach the early to middle fifties, and then draw heavily on the backs of taxpayers for decades more. It is not uncommon for a government worker to draw more pay in retirement than they did during active service.

THE CONFLICT OF INTEREST may be the primary cause of extraordinary salaries and benefits for government workers. It begins when union advocates sit on both sides of the bargaining table, which steps on the rights of private citizens. Government employees can directly influence the management of their activities through political contributions. The private American citizen pays the wages and benefits of government workers through the contribution of taxes. The government worker uses a portion of these wages to pay union dues. The union organization uses a portion of its dues to support the campaign of a particular candidate for political office. In return, the elected official supports the union workers with approval of pay increases, improved health subsidies, and generous retirement programs. All of the pay increases, health care payments, and retirement contributions are at the expense of the private citizen.

Worse, often the government agent, or representative, will benefit from the terms of the contract, too. When government employees receive increases in salaries, improved health care benefits, and generous retirement payouts, both the elected officials and non-union government employees eventually receive a similar raise. Government representatives know this, and so the incentive to keep labor costs in check is squeezed by the lure of union support.

During contract negotiations, government unions are sitting on both sides of the bargaining table, causing a conflict of interest that should be abolished.

THE PRIMARY DISADVANTAGE of union labor is the inherent inefficiency of the whole system. It begins with wages that are inflated by union dues. Taxpayers must absorb the extra costs of bulky contracts, stewards, meetings, and dues. Without these extra costs, the operational costs can be pared substantially.

The government actually pays the union dues in the form of wages, so this extra cost is added to the labor cost structure. Just about every time workers receive a pay increase there is an increase in union dues. Cost structures are swollen further by the additional time and personnel required for union supervision and management. Most unions require stewards and chief stewards to watch over the operation and consult with union members. In some cases these individuals work on the job part time and conduct union business part time. Some contracts require union funds (from union dues paid by the taxpayers) be used to pay for the time spent on union business, but in many situations the government pays the wages for both the steward and worker while they consult in a private area provided by the government. The result of this situation usually means extra workers to cover the time lost while union workers are conducting union business.

Union inefficiencies don't end with dues and more people, though. Union operations typically are slow to react to changing situations. Contracts often don't allow government managers to make swift decisions to meet a crisis or take advantage of an opportunity, because they are restrained by contract provisions and must consult with union officials first. This can slow down reaction time and add cost.

The threat of wasteful strikes looms over taxpayers, too. Strikes bring constant tension that generally infects relationships in an operation working under a union contract. The net result of a strike is a loss for both the workers and the taxpayers. The gains in wages and benefits, which may result from a strike, are usually offset by the lost wages during the strike, and it may take years to recover. Taxpayers suffer with reduced or discontinued services during strikes, but continue to pay taxes, even though services have been lost. No one wins during a strike, but they are often the inevitable result of dealing with a union.

INEQUITABLE WAGES AND BENEFITS are the result of the unceasing push by unions for more power and privilege. Government operations are a cost that must be borne by taxpayers, and it has become completely out of balance.

Today this situation has resulted with government workers earning a higher-than-average salary with extraordinary health care payments and retirement plans. They earn more than the average private citizen. They receive a higher payment of health care premiums than the average private citizen. They receive matching retirement plan contributions higher than the average private citizen, and they can retire earlier with cost-of-living adjustments to their pay that few private pensions offer. They receive more vacation and holidays than the average private citizen. Much of this is the direct result of the contribution of union dues to campaign funds, and the rest is from slack management by elected officials. Worse, the government officials that negotiate these contracts often receive the same benefits for themselves.

GOVERNMENT UNIONS SHOULD BE ABOLISHED, either by legislation or constitutional amendment. This should include provisions for the prohibition of strikes. Unions are not necessarily bad, and at times they are useful in keeping management honest, but the days of unreasonable management have been replaced with a new era of regulations and standards. Unions commonly use security and protection as a justification for their existence. One hundred years ago the country didn't have the employment protection laws of today, so the union movement was necessary to expose this need, but today, the federal laws of the good people of the country assure labor protection. With all of the federal occupational and labor rules, most organizations and managers have been trained to treat the labor force properly and to provide a safe and comfortable working environment. Government workers in particular, can turn to regulations and the good faith of the taxpayers to find the security and protection they currently seek through a union organization.

Government pay and benefits should be adjusted. Government workers should never receive more pay or benefits than the local average for similar skills and responsibilities in the private sector. Routine wage and benefit surveys should be used to control and adjust their compensation packages. If government employment laws establish the compensation packages, then their protection is assured, and the nation is relieved from the threats of union strikes or other misconduct to get its way.

The alternative to abolishing unionization of government jobs would be to turn over the operation to private companies where possible. By using private enterprise to operate government activities, then unions could petition for certification with the private employer. But strikes by public service workers must be prohibited as a condition for employment. Where private operations are impractical or not possible, unions would be abolished. But the American people are entitled to the lowest cost and most efficient operation possible.

Surely, one of the most liberating adjustments by federal and state governments would be to eradicate permissible government unions. These jobs should be returned to conservative levels, and the security of the private citizen must be considered above that of the government employee. If these union members want high pay and extraordinary benefits, they should enter the competitive world.

Note: The historical text of the Constitution has been edited in this copy of contemporary American usage. The format does not specifically conform to the original. For example, clause numbers were not part of the original, but have been included here for the reference of the reader, with other minor variations for convenience.

Constitution of the United States of America

We the People of the United States, in Order to form a more perfect Union, establish Justice, insure domestic Tranquility, provide for the common defence, promote the general Welfare, and secure the Blessings of Liberty to ourselves and our Posterity, do ordain and establish this Constitution for the United States of America.

Article I

Section 1
All legislative Powers herein granted shall be vested in a Congress of the United States, which shall consist of a Senate and House of Representatives.

Section 2
1: The House of Representatives shall be composed of Members chosen every second Year by the People of the several States, and the Electors in each State shall have the Qualifications requisite for Electors of the most numerous Branch of the State Legislature.

2: No Person shall be a Representative who shall not have attained to the Age of twenty five Years, and been seven Years a Citizen of the United States, and who shall not, when elected, be an Inhabitant of that State in which he shall be chosen.

3: Representatives and direct Taxes shall be apportioned among the several States which may be included within this Union, according to their respective Numbers, which shall be determined by adding to the whole Number of free Persons, including those bound to Service for a Term of Years, and excluding Indians not taxed, three fifths of all other Persons. The actual Enumeration shall be made within three Years after the first Meeting of the Congress of the United States, and within every subsequent Term of ten Years, in such Manner as they shall by Law direct. The Number of Representatives shall not exceed one for every thirty Thousand, but each State shall have at Least one Representative; and until such enumeration shall be made, the State of New Hampshire shall be entitled to chuse three, Massachusetts eight, Rhode-Island and Providence Plantations one, Connecticut five, New-York six, New Jersey four, Pennsylvania eight, Delaware one, Maryland six, Virginia ten, North Carolina five, South Carolina five, and Georgia three.

4: When vacancies happen in the Representation from any State, the Executive Authority thereof shall issue Writs of Election to fill such Vacancies.

5: The House of Representatives shall chuse their Speaker and other Officers; and shall have the sole Power of Impeachment.

Section 3

1: The Senate of the United States shall be composed of two Senators from each State, chosen by the Legislature thereof, for six Years; and each Senator shall have one Vote.

2: Immediately after they shall be assembled in Consequence of the first Election, they shall be divided as equally as may be into three Classes. The Seats of the Senators of the first Class shall be vacated at the Expiration of the second Year, of the second Class at the Expiration of the fourth Year, and of the third Class at the Expiration of the sixth Year, so that one third may be chosen every second Year; and if Vacancies happen by Resignation, or otherwise, during the Recess of the Legislature of any State, the Executive thereof may make temporary Appointments until the next Meeting of the Legislature, which shall then fill such Vacancies.

3: No Person shall be a Senator who shall not have attained to the Age of thirty Years, and been nine Years a Citizen of the United States, and who shall not, when elected, be an Inhabitant of that State for which he shall be chosen.

4: The Vice President of the United States shall be President of the Senate, but shall have no Vote, unless they be equally divided.

5: The Senate shall chuse their other Officers, and also a President pro tempore, in the Absence of the Vice President, or when he shall exercise the Office of President of the United States.

6: The Senate shall have the sole Power to try all Impeachments. When sitting for that Purpose, they shall be on Oath or Affirmation. When the President of the United States is tried, the Chief Justice shall preside: And no Person shall be convicted without the Concurrence of two thirds of the Members present.

7: Judgment in Cases of impeachment shall not extend further than to removal from Office, and disqualification to hold and enjoy any Office of honor, Trust or Profit under the United States: but the Party convicted shall nevertheless be liable and subject to Indictment, Trial, Judgment and Punishment, according to Law.

Section 4

1: The Times, Places and Manner of holding Elections for Senators and Representatives, shall be prescribed in each State by the Legislature thereof; but the Congress may at any time by Law make or alter such Regulations, except as to the Places of chusing Senators.

2: The Congress shall assemble at least once in every Year, and such Meeting shall be on the first Monday in December, unless they shall by Law appoint a different Day.

Section 5

1: Each House shall be the Judge of the Elections, Returns and Qualifications of its own Members, and a Majority of each shall constitute a Quorum to do Business; but a smaller Number may adjourn from day to day, and may be authorized to compel the Attendance of absent Members, in such Manner, and under such Penalties as each House may provide.

2: Each House may determine the Rules of its Proceedings, punish its Members for disorderly Behaviour, and, with the Concurrence of two thirds, expel a Member.

3: Each House shall keep a Journal of its Proceedings, and from time to time publish the same, excepting such Parts as may in their Judgment require Secrecy; and the Yeas and Nays of the Members of either House on any question shall, at the Desire of one fifth of those Present, be entered on the Journal.

4: Neither House, during the Session of Congress, shall, without the Consent of the other, adjourn for more than three days, nor to any other Place than that in which the two Houses shall be sitting.

Section 6

1: The Senators and Representatives shall receive a Compensation for their Services, to be ascertained by Law, and paid out of the Treasury of the United States. They shall in all Cases, except Treason, Felony and Breach of the Peace, be privileged from Arrest during their Attendance at the Session of their respective Houses, and in going to and returning from the same; and for any Speech or Debate in either House, they shall not be questioned in any other Place.

2: No Senator or Representative shall, during the Time for which he was elected, be appointed to any civil Office under the Authority of the United States, which shall have been created, or the Emoluments whereof shall have been encreased during such time; and no Person holding any Office under the United States, shall be a Member of either House during his Continuance in Office.

Section 7

1: All Bills for raising Revenue shall originate in the House of Representatives; but the Senate may propose or concur with Amendments as on other Bills.

2: Every Bill which shall have passed the House of Representatives and the Senate, shall, before it become a Law, be presented to the President of the United States; If he approve he shall sign it, but if not he shall return it, with his Objections to that House in which it shall have originated, who shall enter the Objections at large on their Journal, and proceed to reconsider it. If after such Reconsideration two thirds of that House shall agree to pass the Bill, it shall be sent, together with the Objections, to the other House, by which it shall likewise be reconsidered, and if approved by two thirds of that House, it shall become a Law. But in all such Cases the Votes of both Houses shall be determined by yeas and Nays, and the Names of the Persons voting for and against the Bill shall be entered on the Journal of each House respectively. If any Bill shall not be returned by the President within ten Days (Sundays excepted) after it shall have been presented to him, the Same shall be a Law, in like Manner as if he had signed it, unless the Congress by their Adjournment prevent its Return, in which Case it shall not be a Law.

3: Every Order, Resolution, or Vote to which the Concurrence of the Senate and House of Representatives may be necessary (except on a question of Adjournment) shall be presented to the President of the United States; and before the Same shall take Effect, shall be approved by him, or being disapproved by him, shall be repassed by two thirds of the Senate and House of Representatives, according to the Rules and Limitations prescribed in the Case of a Bill.

Section 8

1: The Congress shall have Power To lay and collect Taxes, Duties, Imposts and Excises, to pay the Debts and provide for the common Defence and general Welfare of the United States; but all Duties, Imposts and Excises shall be uniform throughout the United States;

2: To borrow Money on the credit of the United States;

3: To regulate Commerce with foreign Nations, and among the several States, and with the Indian Tribes;

4: To establish an uniform Rule of Naturalization, and uniform Laws on the subject of Bankruptcies throughout the United States;

5: To coin Money, regulate the Value thereof, and of foreign Coin, and fix the Standard of Weights and Measures;

6: To provide for the Punishment of counterfeiting the Securities and current Coin of the United States;

7: To establish Post Offices and post Roads;

8: To promote the Progress of Science and useful Arts, by securing for limited Times to Authors and Inventors the exclusive Right to their respective Writings and Discoveries;

9: To constitute Tribunals inferior to the supreme Court;

10: To define and punish Piracies and Felonies committed on the high Seas, and Offences against the Law of Nations;

11: To declare War, grant Letters of Marque and Reprisal, and make Rules concerning Captures on Land and Water;

12: To raise and support Armies, but no Appropriation of Money to that Use shall be for a longer Term than two Years;

13: To provide and maintain a Navy;

14: To make Rules for the Government and Regulation of the land and naval Forces;

15: To provide for calling forth the Militia to execute the Laws of the Union, suppress Insurrections and repel Invasions;

16: To provide for organizing, arming, and disciplining, the Militia, and for governing such Part of them as may be employed in the Service of the United States, reserving to the States respectively, the Appointment of the Officers, and the Authority of training the Militia according to the discipline prescribed by Congress;

17: To exercise exclusive Legislation in all Cases whatsoever, over such District (not exceeding ten Miles square) as may, by Cession of particular States, and the Acceptance of Congress, become the Seat of the Government of the United States, and to exercise like Authority over all Places purchased by the Consent of the Legislature of the State in which the Same shall be, for the Erection of Forts, Magazines, Arsenals, dock-Yards, and other needful Buildings; And

18: To make all Laws which shall be necessary and proper for carrying into Execution the foregoing Powers, and all other Powers vested by this Constitution in the Government of the United States, or in any Department or Officer thereof.

Section 9

1: The Migration or Importation of such Persons as any of the States now existing shall think proper to admit, shall not be prohibited by the Congress prior to the Year one thousand eight hundred and eight, but a Tax or duty may be imposed on such Importation, not exceeding ten dollars for each Person.

2: The Privilege of the Writ of Habeas Corpus shall not be suspended, unless when in Cases of Rebellion or Invasion the public Safety may require it.

3: No Bill of Attainder or ex post facto Law shall be passed.

4: No Capitation, or other direct, Tax shall be laid, unless in Proportion to the Census or Enumeration herein before directed to be taken.

5: No Tax or Duty shall be laid on Articles exported from any State.

6: No Preference shall be given by any Regulation of Commerce or Revenue to the Ports of one State over those of another: nor shall Vessels bound to, or from, one State, be obliged to enter, clear, or pay Duties in another.

7: No Money shall be drawn from the Treasury, but in Consequence of Appropriations made by Law; and a regular Statement and Account of the Receipts and Expenditures of all public Money shall be published from time to time.

8: No Title of Nobility shall be granted by the United States: And no Person holding any Office of Profit or Trust under them, shall, without the Consent of the Congress, accept of any present, Emolument, Office, or Title, of any kind whatever, from any King, Prince, or foreign State.

Section 10

1: No State shall enter into any Treaty, Alliance, or Confederation; grant Letters of Marque and Reprisal; coin Money; emit Bills of Credit; make any Thing but gold and silver Coin a Tender in Payment of Debts; pass any Bill of Attainder, ex post facto Law, or Law impairing the Obligation of Contracts, or grant any Title of Nobility.

2: No State shall, without the Consent of the Congress, lay any Imposts or Duties on Imports or Exports, except what may be absolutely necessary for executing it's inspection Laws: and the net Produce of all Duties and Imposts, laid by any State on Imports or Exports, shall be for the Use of the Treasury of the United States; and all such Laws shall be subject to the Revision and Controul of the Congress.

3: No State shall, without the Consent of Congress, lay any Duty of Tonnage, keep Troops, or Ships of War in time of Peace, enter into any Agreement or Compact with another State, or with a foreign Power, or engage in War, unless actually invaded, or in such imminent Danger as will not admit of delay.

Article II

Section 1

1: The executive Power shall be vested in a President of the United States of America. He shall hold his Office during the Term of four Years, and, together with the Vice President, chosen for the same Term, be elected, as follows

2: Each State shall appoint, in such Manner as the Legislature thereof may direct, a Number of Electors, equal to the whole Number of Senators and

Representatives to which the State may be entitled in the Congress: but no Senator or Representative, or Person holding an Office of Trust or Profit under the United States, shall be appointed an Elector.

3: The Electors shall meet in their respective States, and vote by Ballot for two Persons, of whom one at least shall not be an Inhabitant of the same State with themselves. And they shall make a List of all the Persons voted for, and of the Number of Votes for each; which List they shall sign and certify, and transmit sealed to the Seat of the Government of the United States, directed to the President of the Senate. The President of the Senate shall, in the Presence of the Senate and House of Representatives, open all the Certificates, and the Votes shall then be counted. The Person having the greatest Number of Votes shall be the President, if such Number be a Majority of the whole Number of Electors appointed; and if there be more than one who have such Majority, and have an equal Number of Votes, then the House of Representatives shall immediately chuse by Ballot one of them for President; and if no Person have a Majority, then from the five highest on the List the said House shall in like Manner chuse the President. But in chusing the President, the Votes shall be taken by States, the Representation from each State having one Vote; A quorum for this Purpose shall consist of a Member or Members from two thirds of the States, and a Majority of all the States shall be necessary to a Choice. In every Case, after the Choice of the President, the Person having the greatest Number of Votes of the Electors shall be the Vice President. But if there should remain two or more who have equal Votes, the Senate shall chuse from them by Ballot the Vice President.

4: The Congress may determine the Time of chusing the Electors, and the Day on which they shall give their Votes; which Day shall be the same throughout the United States.

5: No Person except a natural born Citizen, or a Citizen of the United States, at the time of the Adoption of this Constitution, shall be eligible to the Office of President; neither shall any Person be eligible to that Office who shall not have attained to the Age of thirty five Years, and been fourteen Years a Resident within the United States.

6: In Case of the Removal of the President from Office, or of his Death, Resignation, or Inability to discharge the Powers and Duties of the said Office, the Same shall devolve on the Vice President, and the Congress may by Law provide for the Case of Removal, Death, Resignation or Inability, both of the President and Vice President, declaring what Officer shall then act as President, and such Officer shall act accordingly, until the Disability be removed, or a President shall be elected.

7: The President shall, at stated Times, receive for his Services, a Compensation, which shall neither be encreased nor diminished during the Period for which he shall have been elected, and he shall not receive within that Period any other Emolument from the United States, or any of them.

8: Before he enter on the Execution of his Office, he shall take the following Oath or Affirmation: "I do solemnly swear (or affirm) that I will faithfully execute the Office of President of the United States, and will to the best of my Ability, preserve, protect and defend the Constitution of the United States."

Section 2

1: The President shall be Commander in Chief of the Army and Navy of the United States, and of the Militia of the several States, when called into the actual Service of the United States; he may require the Opinion, in writing, of the principal Officer in each of the executive Departments, upon any Subject relating to the Duties of their respective Offices, and he shall have Power to grant Reprieves and Pardons for Offences against the United States, except in Cases of Impeachment.

2: He shall have Power, by and with the Advice and Consent of the Senate, to make Treaties, provided two thirds of the Senators present concur; and he shall nominate, and by and with the Advice and Consent of the Senate, shall appoint Ambassadors, other public Ministers and Consuls, Judges of the supreme Court, and all other Officers of the United States, whose Appointments are not herein otherwise provided for, and which shall be established by Law: but the Congress may by Law vest the Appointment of such inferior Officers, as they think proper, in the President alone, in the Courts of Law, or in the Heads of Departments.

3: The President shall have Power to fill up all Vacancies that may happen during the Recess of the Senate, by granting Commissions which shall expire at the End of their next Session.

Section 3

He shall from time to time give to the Congress Information of the State of the Union, and recommend to their Consideration such Measures as he shall judge necessary and expedient; he may, on extraordinary Occasions, convene both Houses, or either of them, and in Case of Disagreement between them, with Respect to the Time of Adjournment, he may adjourn them to such Time as he shall think proper; he shall receive Ambassadors and other public Ministers; he shall take Care that the Laws be faithfully executed, and shall Commission all the Officers of the United States.

Section 4

The President, Vice President and all civil Officers of the United States, shall be removed from Office on Impeachment for, and Conviction of, Treason, Bribery, or other high Crimes and Misdemeanors.

Article III

Section 1

The judicial Power of the United States, shall be vested in one supreme Court, and in such inferior Courts as the Congress may from time to time ordain and establish. The Judges, both of the supreme and inferior Courts, shall hold their Offices during good Behaviour, and shall, at stated Times, receive for their Services, a Compensation, which shall not be diminished during their Continuance in Office.

Section 2

1: The judicial Power shall extend to all Cases, in Law and Equity, arising under this Constitution, the Laws of the United States, and Treaties made, or which shall be made, under their Authority; to all Cases affecting Ambassadors, other public Ministers and Consuls; to all Cases of admiralty and maritime Jurisdiction; to Controversies to which the United States shall be a Party; to Controversies between two or more States; between a State and Citizens of another State; between Citizens of different States, between Citizens of the same State claiming Lands under Grants of different States, and between a State, or the Citizens thereof, and foreign States, Citizens or Subjects.

2: In all Cases affecting Ambassadors, other public Ministers and Consuls, and those in which a State shall be Party, the supreme Court shall have original Jurisdiction. In all the other Cases before mentioned, the supreme Court shall have appellate Jurisdiction, both as to Law and Fact, with such Exceptions, and under such Regulations as the Congress shall make.

3: The Trial of all Crimes, except in Cases of Impeachment, shall be by Jury; and such Trial shall be held in the State where the said Crimes shall have been committed; but when not committed within any State, the Trial shall be at such Place or Places as the Congress may by Law have directed.

Section 3

1: Treason against the United States, shall consist only in levying War against them, or in adhering to their Enemies, giving them Aid and Comfort. No Person shall be convicted of Treason unless on the Testimony of two Witnesses to the same overt Act, or on Confession in open Court.

2: The Congress shall have Power to declare the Punishment of Treason, but no Attainder of Treason shall work Corruption of Blood, or Forfeiture except during the Life of the Person attainted.

Article IV

Section 1

Full Faith and Credit shall be given in each State to the public Acts, Records, and judicial Proceedings of every other State. And the Congress may by general Laws prescribe the Manner in which such Acts, Records and Proceedings shall be proved, and the Effect thereof.

Section 2

1: The Citizens of each State shall be entitled to all Privileges and Immunities of Citizens in the several States.

2: A Person charged in any State with Treason, Felony, or other Crime, who shall flee from Justice, and be found in another State, shall on Demand of the executive Authority of the State from which he fled, be delivered up, to be removed to the State having Jurisdiction of the Crime.

3: No Person held to Service or Labour in one State, under the Laws thereof, escaping into another, shall, in Consequence of any Law or Regulation therein, be discharged from such Service or Labour, but shall be delivered up on Claim of the Party to whom such Service or Labour may be due.

Section 3

1: New States may be admitted by the Congress into this Union; but no new State shall be formed or erected within the Jurisdiction of any other State; nor any State be formed by the Junction of two or more States, or Parts of States, without the Consent of the Legislatures of the States concerned as well as of the Congress.

2: The Congress shall have Power to dispose of and make all needful Rules and Regulations respecting the Territory or other Property belonging to the United States; and nothing in this Constitution shall be so construed as to Prejudice any Claims of the United States, or of any particular State.

Section 4

The United States shall guarantee to every State in this Union a Republican Form of Government, and shall protect each of them against Invasion; and on Application of the Legislature, or of the Executive (when the Legislature cannot be convened) against domestic Violence.

Article V

The Congress, whenever two thirds of both Houses shall deem it necessary, shall propose Amendments to this Constitution, or, on the Application of the Legislatures of two thirds of the several States, shall call a Convention for proposing Amendments, which, in either Case, shall be valid to all Intents and Purposes, as Part of this Constitution, when ratified by the Legislatures of three fourths of the several States, or by Conventions in three fourths thereof, as the one or the other Mode of Ratification may be proposed by the Congress; Provided that no Amendment which may be made prior to the Year One thousand eight hundred and eight shall in any Manner affect the first and fourth Clauses in the Ninth Section of the first Article; and that no State, without its Consent, shall be deprived of its equal Suffrage in the Senate.

Article VI

1: All Debts contracted and Engagements entered into, before the Adoption of this Constitution, shall be as valid against the United States under this Constitution, as under the Confederation.

2: This Constitution, and the Laws of the United States which shall be made in Pursuance thereof; and all Treaties made, or which shall be made, under the Authority of the United States, shall be the supreme Law of the Land; and the Judges in every State shall be bound thereby, any Thing in the Constitution or Laws of any State to the Contrary notwithstanding.

3: The Senators and Representatives before mentioned, and the Members of the several State Legislatures, and all executive and judicial Officers, both of the United States and of the several States, shall be bound by Oath or Affirmation, to support this Constitution; but no religious Test shall ever be required as a Qualification to any Office or public Trust under the United States.

Article VII

The Ratification of the Conventions of nine States, shall be sufficient for the Establishment of this Constitution between the States so ratifying the Same.

Done in Convention by the Unanimous Consent of the States present the Seventeenth Day of September in the Year of our Lord one thousand seven hundred and Eighty seven and of the Independence of the United States of America the Twelfth. In witness whereof We have hereunto subscribed our Names,

Amendments to the Constitution

Amendment I

Congress shall make no law respecting an establishment of religion, or prohibiting the free exercise thereof; or abridging the freedom of speech, or of the press; or the right of the people peaceably to assemble, and to petition the Government for a redress of grievances.

Amendment II

A well regulated Militia, being necessary to the security of a free State, the right of the people to keep and bear Arms, shall not be infringed.

Amendment III

No Soldier shall, in time of peace be quartered in any house, without the consent of the Owner, nor in time of war, but in a manner to be prescribed by law.

Amendment IV

The right of the people to be secure in their persons, houses, papers, and effects, against unreasonable searches and seizures, shall not be violated, and no Warrants shall issue, but upon probable cause, supported by Oath or affirmation, and particularly describing the place to be searched, and the persons or things to be seized.

Amendment V

No person shall be held to answer for a capital, or otherwise infamous crime, unless on a presentment or indictment of a Grand Jury, except in cases arising in the land or naval forces, or in the Militia, when in actual service in time of War or public danger; nor shall any person be subject for the same offence to be twice put in jeopardy of life or limb; nor shall be compelled in any criminal case to be a witness against himself, nor be deprived of life, liberty, or property, without due process of law; nor shall private property be taken for public use, without just compensation.

Amendment VI

In all criminal prosecutions, the accused shall enjoy the right to a speedy and public trial, by an impartial jury of the State and district wherein the crime shall have been committed, which district shall have been previously ascertained by law, and to be informed of the nature and cause of the accusation; to be confronted with the witnesses against him; to have compulsory process for obtaining witnesses in his favor, and to have the Assistance of Counsel for his defence.

Amendment VII

In Suits at common law, where the value in controversy shall exceed twenty dollars, the right of trial by jury shall be preserved, and no fact tried by a jury, shall be otherwise re-examined in any Court of the United States, than according to the rules of the common law.

Amendment VIII

Excessive bail shall not be required, nor excessive fines imposed, nor cruel and unusual punishments inflicted.

Amendment IX

The enumeration in the Constitution, of certain rights, shall not be construed to deny or disparage others retained by the people.

Amendment X

The powers not delegated to the United States by the Constitution, nor prohibited by it to the States, are reserved to the States respectively, or to the people.

Amendment XI

The Judicial power of the United States shall not be construed to extend to any suit in law or equity, commenced or prosecuted against one of the United States by Citizens of another State, or by Citizens or Subjects of any Foreign State.

Amendment XII

The Electors shall meet in their respective states, and vote by ballot for President and Vice-President, one of whom, at least, shall not be an inhabitant of the same state with themselves; they shall name in their ballots the person voted for as President, and in distinct ballots the person voted for as Vice-President, and they shall make distinct lists of all persons voted for as President, and of all persons voted for as Vice-President, and of the number of votes for each, which lists they shall sign and certify, and transmit sealed to the seat of the government of the United States, directed to the President of the Senate; The President of the Senate shall, in the presence of the Senate and House of Representatives, open all the certificates and the votes shall then be counted; The person having the greatest number of votes for President, shall be the President, if such number be a majority of the whole number of Electors appointed; and if no person have such majority, then from the persons having the highest numbers not exceeding three on the list of those voted for as President, the House of Representatives shall choose immediately, by ballot, the President. But in choosing the President, the votes shall be taken by states, the representation from each state having one vote; a quorum for this purpose shall consist of a member or members from two-thirds of the states, and a majority of all the states shall be necessary to a choice. And if the House of Representatives shall not choose a President whenever the right of choice shall devolve upon them, before the fourth day of March next following, then the Vice-President shall act as President, as in the case of the death or other constitutional disability of the President. The person having the greatest number of votes as Vice-President, shall be the Vice-President, if such number be a majority of the whole number of Electors appointed, and if no person have a majority, then from the two highest numbers on the list, the Senate shall choose the Vice-President; a quorum for the purpose shall consist of two-thirds of the whole number of Senators, and a majority of the whole number shall be necessary to a choice. But no person constitutionally ineligible to the office of President shall be eligible to that of Vice-President of the United States.

Amendment XIII

Neither slavery nor involuntary servitude, except as a punishment for crime whereof the party shall have been duly convicted, shall exist within the United States, or any place subject to their jurisdiction.

Congress shall have power to enforce this article by appropriate legislation.

Amendment XIV

Section 1: All persons born or naturalized in the United States, and subject to the jurisdiction thereof, are citizens of the United States and of the State wherein they reside. No State shall make or enforce any law which shall abridge the privileges or immunities of citizens of the United States; nor shall any State deprive any person of life, liberty, or property, without due process of law; nor deny to any person within its jurisdiction the equal protection of the laws.

Section 2: Representatives shall be apportioned among the several States according to their respective numbers, counting the whole number of persons in each State, excluding Indians not taxed. But when the right to vote at any election for the choice of electors for President and Vice President of the United States, Representatives in Congress, the Executive and Judicial officers of a State, or the members of the Legislature thereof, is denied to any of the male inhabitants of such State, being twenty-one years of age, and citizens of the United States, or in any way abridged, except for participation in rebellion, or other crime, the basis of representation therein shall be reduced in the proportion which the number of such male citizens shall bear to the whole number of male citizens twenty-one years of age in such State.

Section 3: No person shall be a Senator or Representative in Congress, or elector of President and Vice President, or hold any office, civil or military, under the United States, or under any State, who, having previously taken an oath, as a member of Congress, or as an officer of the United States, or as a member of any State legislature, or as an executive or judicial officer of any State, to support the Constitution of the United States, shall have engaged in insurrection or rebellion against the same, or given aid or comfort to the enemies thereof. But Congress may by a vote of two-thirds of each House, remove such disability.

Section 4: The validity of the public debt of the United States, authorized by law, including debts incurred for payment of pensions and bounties for services in suppressing insurrection or rebellion, shall not be questioned. But neither the United States nor any State shall assume or pay any debt or obligation incurred in aid of insurrection or rebellion against the United States, or any claim for the loss or emancipation of any slave; but all such debts, obligations and claims shall be held illegal and void.

Section 5: The Congress shall have power to enforce, by appropriate legislation, the provisions of this article.

Amendment XV

The right of citizens of the United States to vote shall not be denied or abridged by the United States or by any State on account of race, color, or previous condition of servitude.

The Congress shall have power to enforce this article by appropriate legislation.

Amendment XVI

The Congress shall have power to lay and collect taxes on incomes, from whatever source derived, without apportionment among the several States, and without regard to any census or enumeration.

Amendment XVII

Section 1: The Senate of the United States shall be composed of two Senators from each State, elected by the people thereof, for six years; and each Senator shall have one vote. The electors in each State shall have the qualifications requisite for electors of the most numerous branch of the State legislatures.

Section 2: When vacancies happen in the representation of any State in the Senate, the executive authority of such State shall issue writs of election to fill such vacancies: Provided, That the legislature of any State may empower the executive thereof to make temporary appointments until the people fill the vacancies by election as the legislature may direct.

Section 3: This amendment shall not be so construed as to affect the election or term of any Senator chosen before it becomes valid as part of the Constitution.

Amendment XVIII

Section 1: After one year from the ratification of this article the manufacture, sale, or transportation of intoxicating liquors within, the importation thereof into, or the exportation thereof from the United States and all territory subject to the jurisdiction thereof for beverage purposes is hereby prohibited.

Section 2: The Congress and the several States shall have concurrent power to enforce this article by appropriate legislation.

Section 3: This article shall be inoperative unless it shall have been ratified as an amendment to the Constitution by the legislatures of the several States, as provided in the Constitution, within seven years from the date of the submission hereof to the States by the Congress.

Amendment XIX

The right of citizens of the United States to vote shall not be denied or abridged by the United States or by any State on account of sex.

Congress shall have power to enforce this article by appropriate legislation.

Amendment XX

Section 1: The terms of the President and Vice President shall end at noon on the 20th day of January, and the terms of Senators and Representatives at noon on the 3d day of January, of the years in which such terms would have ended if this article had not been ratified; and the terms of their successors shall then begin.

Section 2: The Congress shall assemble at least once in every year, and such meeting shall begin at noon on the 3d day of January, unless they shall by law appoint a different day.

Section 3: If, at the time fixed for the beginning of the term of the President, the President elect shall have died, the Vice President elect shall become President. If a President shall not have been chosen before the time fixed for the beginning of his term, or if the President elect shall have failed to qualify, then the Vice President elect shall act as President until a President shall have qualified; and the Congress may by law provide for the case wherein neither a President elect nor a Vice President elect shall have qualified, declaring who shall then act as President, or the manner in which one who is to act shall be selected, and such person shall act accordingly until a President or Vice President shall have qualified.

Section 4: The Congress may by law provide for the case of the death of any of the persons from whom the House of Representatives may choose a President whenever the right of choice shall have devolved upon them, and for the case of the death of any of the persons from whom the Senate may choose a Vice President whenever the right of choice shall have devolved upon them.

Section 5: Sections 1 and 2 shall take effect on the 15th day of October following the ratification of this article.

Section 6: This article shall be inoperative unless it shall have been ratified as an amendment to the Constitution by the legislatures of three-fourths of the several States within seven years from the date of its submission.

Amendment XXI

Section 1: The eighteenth article of amendment to the Constitution of the United States is hereby repealed.

Section 2: The transportation or importation into any State, Territory, or possession of the United States for delivery or use therein of intoxicating liquors, in violation of the laws thereof, is hereby prohibited.

Section 3: This article shall be inoperative unless it shall have been ratified as an amendment to the Constitution by conventions in the several States, as provided in the Constitution, within seven years from the date of the submission hereof to the States by the Congress.

Amendment XXII

Section 1: No person shall be elected to the office of the President more than twice, and no person who has held the office of President, or acted as President, for more than two years of a term to which some other person was elected President shall be elected to the office of the President more than once. But this article shall not apply to any person holding the office of President when this article was proposed by the Congress, and shall not prevent any person who may be holding the office of President, or acting as President, during the term within which this article becomes operative from holding the office of President or acting as President during the remainder of such term.

Section 2: This article shall be inoperative unless it shall have been ratified as an amendment to the Constitution by the legislatures of three-fourths of the several states within seven years from the date of its submission to the states by the Congress.

Amendment XXIII

Section 1: The District constituting the seat of government of the United States shall appoint in such manner as the Congress may direct: A number of electors of President and Vice President equal to the whole number of Senators and Representatives in Congress to which the District would be entitled if it were a state, but in no event more than the least populous state; they shall be in addition to those appointed by the states, but they shall be considered, for the purposes of the election of President and Vice President, to be electors appointed by a state; and they shall meet in the District and perform such duties as provided by the twelfth article of amendment.

Section 2: The Congress shall have power to enforce this article by appropriate legislation.

Amendment XXIV

Section 1. The right of citizens of the United States to vote in any primary or other election for President or Vice President, for electors for President or Vice President, or for Senator or Representative in Congress, shall not be denied or abridged by the United States or any state by reason of failure to pay any poll tax or other tax.

Section 2. The Congress shall have power to enforce this article by appropriate legislation.

Amendment XXV

Section 1: In case of the removal of the President from office or of his death or resignation, the Vice President shall become President.

Section 2: Whenever there is a vacancy in the office of the Vice President, the President shall nominate a Vice President who shall take office upon confirmation by a majority vote of both Houses of Congress.

Section 3: Whenever the President transmits to the President pro tempore of the Senate and the Speaker of the House of Representatives his written declaration that he is unable to discharge the powers and duties of his office, and until he transmits to them a written declaration to the contrary, such powers and duties shall be discharged by the Vice President as Acting President.

Section 4: Whenever the Vice President and a majority of either the principal officers of the executive departments or of such other body as Congress may by law provide, transmit to the President pro tempore of the Senate and the Speaker of the House of Representatives their written declaration that the President is unable to discharge the powers and duties of his office, the Vice President shall immediately assume the powers and duties of the office as Acting President.

Thereafter, when the President transmits to the President pro tempore of the Senate and the Speaker of the House of Representatives his written declaration that no inability exists, he shall resume the powers and duties of his office unless the Vice President and a majority of either the principal officers of the executive department or of such other body as Congress may by law provide, transmit within four days to the President pro tempore of the Senate and the Speaker of the House of Representatives their written declaration that the President is unable to discharge the powers and duties of his office. Thereupon Congress shall decide the issue, assembling within forty-eight hours for that purpose if not in session. If the Congress, within twenty-one days after receipt of the latter written declaration, or, if Congress is not in session, within twenty-one days after Congress is required to assemble, determines by two-thirds vote of both Houses that the President is unable to discharge the powers and duties of his office, the Vice President shall continue to discharge the same as Acting President; otherwise, the President shall resume the powers and duties of his office.

Amendment XXVI

Section 1: The right of citizens of the United States, who are 18 years of age or older, to vote, shall not be denied or abridged by the United States or any state on account of age.

Section 2: The Congress shall have the power to enforce this article by appropriate legislation.

Amendment XXVII

No law varying the compensation for the services of the Senators and Representatives shall take effect until an election of Representatives shall have intervened.

About the Author

Raised in the Southwest United States, the author has been active in engineering and business since the 1960s. His career includes service in the US Army, engineering and accounting assignments, and senior technical management responsibilities. Hobbies are aviation and flight instruction, reading, and writing. His range of writing includes magazine articles and books covering fiction and nonfiction subjects for adults and children.